PENNSYLVANIA AVENUE

AMERICA'S MAIN STREET

PENNSYLVANIA AVENUE
AMERICA'S MAIN STREET

Carol M. Highsmith and Ted Landphair
Featuring the Photographs of Carol M. Highsmith
Foreword by Daniel Patrick Moynihan

The American Institute of Architects Press
Washington, D.C.

The American Institute of Architects Press
1735 New York Avenue, N.W.
Washington, D.C. 20006

93   92   91   90   89   88   5   4   3   2   1

ISBN 1-55835-000-4

ISBN 1-55835-010-1 (pbk)

Library of Congress Cataloging-in-Publication Data

Highsmith, Carol M., 1946–
    Pennsylvania Avenue: America's main street / by Carol M. Highsmith and Ted
Landphair; featuring the photographs of Carol M. Highsmith
        p.   cm.
    Bibliography: p.
    Includes index.
    ISBN 1–588–35000–4: $39.95 (est.). ISBN 1–558–35010–1 (pbk.): $29.95 (est.)
    1. Pennsylvania Avenue (Washington, D.C.) 2. Washington, D.C. — History. I.
Landphair, Ted, 1942–   . II. Title.
F203.7.P4H54 1988
975.3–dc19   88–22279
                                                                                CIP

Design by Meadows & Wiser, Washington, D.C.
Composition in Century Expanded by General Typographers, Inc.,
Washington, D.C.
Color separation by Graphic Technology and Information, New York
Printing by D.W. Friesen & Sons, Winnipeg, through Four-Colour Imports,
Louisville

Frontispiece: The refreshed Hotel Washington (note sgraffito detail on facade
depicting famous Americans and Masonic symbols), Willard Hotel, Pennsylvania
Building, and Old Post Office. Although the P.O. was restored in the early 1980s,
it was again covered with scaffolding in this 1987 view. Why? The roof was being
reslated, a project that required eighteen months and considerable temerity.
Because of high winds near the apogee of the 315-foot-tall belfry, the scaffolding
took nine months to erect and three months to dismantle. (Carol M. Highsmith)

Acknowledgments   7

Foreword by Daniel Patrick Moynihan   8

Introduction   12

AN AVENUE FIELD GUIDE

From the White House to Freedom Plaza   18

From Freedom Plaza to Market Square   26

To the Capitol   36

WHAT'S PAST IS PROLOGUE

Slop on the Avenue   50

Charnel Along the Tiber and a Road Made of Iron   60

Shucking at Harvey's and Jiving at Kann's   74

Pathway of the Presidents   86

THE ERA OF RECONSTRUCTION

Monumental Undertakings   104

Oh Lost! And By the Wind Grieved!   114

Life and Transfiguration   132

WITNESSES TO THE PASSING OF TIME

Proud as a Peacock Again   160

Cheating the Wrecker's Ball   170

Epilogue: Your Main Street   181

Suggested Reading List   185

Index   186

To Dorothy M. Jones,
friend of both the authors
and of Pennsylvania Avenue,
indefatigable contributor
to this volume,
and wise counselor
in the ways of humankind.

Acknowledgments

Pennsylvania Avenue's ceremonial core is a relatively short strip — but because of its national significance and rich lore, the intertwining jurisdictions that affect it, and its entangled legacy of prosperity and deterioration, it's a bear of a road for a researcher to get hold of. Thus, those who study the Avenue must rely upon the kindness of many people in order to make readable sense out of it.

The authors are indebted to historians Frederick Gutheim and James A. Goode for their encouragement, guidance, and personal reminiscences, not to mention their eloquent writing that provided bedrock information on the Avenue. The remarkable Professor Gutheim's direct contribution to the revitalization of Pennsylvania Avenue extended all the way from his studies of L'Enfant and many other grand plans, to his own contributions on (and backstage of) the first presidential commission to attempt an Avenue rehabilitation. Because the authors are neither architects nor students of matters like creek topography, they are grateful, too, to Washington architect Donald A. Hawkins for setting them on — and occasionally back on — course in their interpretation of the Avenue's early days.

Chairmen, executive directors, and key staff, present and past, of the Pennsylvania Avenue Development Corporation were uniformly helpful in opening their files, jiggling their memories, and providing leads to additional information. In particular, Chairman Henry A. Berliner; Executive Director Jay Brodie; Design Director Yong-Duk Chyun; and Anne Hartzell, PADC's director of corporate affairs and congressional relations, encouraged and facilitated the research.

Many other important contributors to the story of the great boulevard also opened their homes, offices, and files to ensure that the story was complete. Recollections of direct players like Pete Quesada, John Woodbridge, Charles A. Horsky, Peter Meszoly, David Childs, Robert Peck, Hugh Newell Jacobsen, Ben Gilbert, and Paul Thiry — unvarnished by concern over how they might ultimately look in print — were offered in the name of telling a fascinating American story. Woodbridge, in particular, took considerable time away from a busy California practice to offer his remembrances. LeRoy O. King, Jr. graciously opened his treasure-trove streetcar collection to this project. John Fondersmith, a talented District of Columbia planner, supplied both wise interpretation of past events and many valuable files.

Design director Robert Wiser, editor Michael Leccese, and copy editor Claudia Ringel "lived" this book with the authors, adding dash, giving it its distinctive look, and watching for forests while the authors stood mesmerized by trees. Carol M. Highsmith's associate, David Patterson, not only helped the photographer capture memorable shots of a great Avenue, he also held her commercial-photography fort with great distinction during the time that this project consumed her. The richness and clarity of many photographs, both historic and current, are due to the fastidious attention of photo-lab technician John Anderson. Research assistant Louisa Papageorge tracked down some of the most important, at times obscure, observers of the passing Avenue scene. Elisabeth M. Hartgens and Susan Hormuth of Imagefinders, Inc., unearthed buried photographic nuggets that greatly accented the historical sections. Librarians from as far away as the Lyndon B. Johnson Library in Texas were helpful, but Steve Ostrow and Mary Ison at the Library of Congress photo division, Roxanna Dean of the Washingtoniana Collection at the Martin Luther King Library, and Lawrence Baum of the Columbia Historical Society in Washington went well beyond professional courtesy to facilitate both the textual and photographic research.

The story of Pennsylvania Avenue is one that they all agreed needed to be told with panache, and their selfless assistance made possible the authors' efforts toward that end.

Foreword

It is ironic that as late twentieth-century American architecture has triumphed, city planning has come to be seen as a thwarted if not failed enterprise. In a general way I think this can be explained. It is all there in Louis Sullivan's remark that the Chicago Exposition of 1893 set back American architecture by half a century. He was quite wrong. American architecture was just then beginning; he himself in the vanguard. It would shortly, as these things go, emerge as the first *international* style in this most central of the arts.

It was city planning, the City Beautiful of those Greek temples on the shore of Lake Michigan, that got lost. How so? Again, a general explanation seems available. Architecture since Palladio has been an intensely individualistic art, and never more than in this century and in this most individualistic of cultures. City planning, for all the brilliant exceptions, tends to be done by committees: committees of the, well . . . cultured. Lots of entropy there.

The more then we ought to welcome this definitive account of Pennsylvania Avenue by Carol M. Highsmith and Ted Landphair, with Highsmith's stunning photography. This is a history of America's Main Street and of the successive committees that rebuilt it in the quarter century between 1963 and 1988. It happens I was present at the outset of this period of revitalization and was more or less continuously involved until the conclusion. It is both an honor and a pleasure, then, to be asked to set down some opening thoughts.

First of all let me assert that the revitalization effort succeeded, if only in the sense that it turned out the way those who got it started *wanted* it to turn out. Let us be spared the charge that the outcome is a jumble of styles and magnitudes and purposes. That was the idea to begin with. It happens that I wrote the initial charter or, if you like, commission, which was included in a document with the unpromising title *Report to the President by the Ad Hoc Committee on Federal Office Space* (1962). There were two parts, actually. First, a federal architectural policy, a one-page affair with a simple message: Be contemporary; avoid an official style. If today that seems unremarkable, even uninspiring, it was something of a manifesto in 1962.

At that point the federal government had not built a contemporary building in Washington in two generations. Our best work, the Federal Triangle begun by Andrew Mellon in the 1920s and unfinished, was unabashedly Chicago Exposition. In the 1930s Eliel and Eero Saarinen almost got to design a museum on Constitution Avenue, but wiser counsel prevailed, and the nearest Eero Saarinen (the younger) got was Dulles Airport — twenty years later and twenty-one miles distant. But there it was: incomparable. In New York there was Mies van der Rohe's Seagram Building. It was so *clear* that we were in a great age and that Washington was missing it. Hence the rule: Build whatever is being built at the time. The U.S. government had in mind to be around for a bit. We would get the good with bad if at any given time we got what was going.

I used to summarize for the benefit of federal planners: At any given moment build whatever the Whiskey Trust is building. But there was also the second proposition: Avoid an official style. This mattered most to me and to those with whom I was closest at the beginning of the enterprise. Recall that this was the age of Brasilia, not to mention the assorted Stalin-allées of the totalitarian world. The Avenue was heading that way. In the last of the Eisenhower years, J. Edgar Hoover got the first new government building to be authorized for the Avenue in four decades: the massive FBI building between Ninth and Tenth streets. Moreover, it was to be on the north side of the Avenue. The prospect was elemental. With a tremendous pressure for new government office space (almost nothing had been started since Mellon's Federal Triangle, which just plain stopped with the onset of the depression), Pennsylvania Avenue was in danger of soon being lined on either side with government buildings. A political statement of huge consequence would have come into being. Even with the best will in the world. Consider the plans Nelson Rockefeller was even then conjuring up for the environs of the New York State capital in Albany. The architecture, as Robert Hughes would write, of coercion. Go see. Try ascending the steps to The Governor Nelson A. Rockefeller Empire State Plaza (sic). Walk south past the gauntlet of looming, indifferent towers toward the sacrificial pyramid at the far end. Man, in the Presence of the State, Thou Art Nothing.

No sooner had early autos appeared than gas-powered tour buses started rumbling up the Avenue. In 1905, this sightseeing company was located where verdant Pershing Park now refreshes pedestrians with its fountains and bosques. (James M. Goode Collection, Library of Congress)

That is what we wanted to prevent, and we did. *You don't have to have a pass to get onto Pennsylvania Avenue.* It is pretty much as envisioned in the specific section on the Avenue in the *Report of the Ad Hoc Committee:* "Pennsylvania Avenue should be lively, friendly and inviting, as well as dignified and impressive."

It is. A jumble, yes; but wonderfully open to people and events. Is there a "body language" to a street? I suppose so. But then I just said so: "the architecture of coercion." Well, ours is a different language. The signs are everywhere: Come On In For Lunch . . . Have A Look! . . . Buy A Book . . . Check Out The Constitution. Yes, there is a good deal of See Me! But why not? Whatever we were, the half dozen of us who began the enterprise, we were in love with people, and this place. We had, you see, won an election!

We were lucky in that, and more. Most of all in the extraordinary talents who joined us as the years went by. Some would not even think themselves involved. For instance, those grand folk who in-

vented the "recycling" of old buildings. Surely, it was just that: an invention. To see what it changed, look in at the Old Post Office, at Twelfth Street. One of the very first things we decided in 1962 was not to tear down that wonderful Romanesque cathedral, which was abandoned and empty save for the flying creatures in the tower and which would have long since vanished had Black Tuesday of 1929 not brought a halt to construction of the Federal Triangle. Apart from a certain contrariness ("they just don't make buildings like that anymore"), our purpose was to preserve the view from the tower. Two hundred and sixty-five feet up, the tower's masonry is broken by a Romanesque colonnade on each of the four sides which presents a stunning panorama of the whole of the city, and, of course, the Avenue. (The only comparison, and it is no equivalent, is the view from the tiny slits at the top of the Washington Monument.) On at least three occasions that I recall, Nat Owings and I risked, if not our lives, then surely our reputation, ascending an endless Pirenesian fantasia of rickety catwalks and dung-layered spiral staircases, only to break out onto that startling view. Now, the view *is* open to the public — via a much more safe, albeit mundane, route — an elevator — and the Old Post Office itself, a vast interior space, is a dazzling world of restaurants and shops and promenades. Something we had never imagined.

We were lucky in our critics. Owings, whose work was Pennsylvania Avenue — it became his life — was curiously old-fashioned for the surviving member of the partnership which made Skidmore Owings & Merrill and modernism synonymous terms the world over. He claimed to have worked on the Commerce Department Building of the Federal Triangle, and did dearly love a grand vista. This, of course, gave him his innate feeling for L'Enfant's city plan. It also got him into planning some plazas the size of which would have given the Renaissance pause and reminded more than a few Washingtonians what the summer heat is like. Peace. They never happened.

We were lucky in people willing to take us at our word that something important was afoot. I think of a succession of owners of the Willard who first wanted to give it to us to tear down and then, wishing to do that themselves, had to hear our entreaties not to. I think especially of Charles Benenson. An eminently sensible and successful developer, he purchased the abandoned building to use the site for an office tower. (Have I mentioned that when this all began, most of Pennsylvania Avenue was abandoned?) This was 1969 and I had become assistant to the president for urban affairs. I asked Mr. Benenson to my White House office, explained that there was a plan for redeveloping the Avenue — nothing exactly to point to, but there was a plan — and that we would very much appreciate his not tearing down the Willard Hotel. Fair enough, he said, but in that event he would like to sell it. Have no fear, I assured him, seeing him out the door where the marine saluted.

For the next two years he would call on me from time to time, explaining that it was costing him a million dollars a month, or some such thing, to leave the building just standing there. Fear not, I repeated. He never showed a moment's impatience and, as far as I know, never once complained that we had cost him a small fortune. They should name a

drink for him at the newly reopened Round Robin Bar.

We were riotously lucky to have our endeavors coincide with the great reign of S. Dillon Ripley as secretary of the Smithsonian. The "nation's attic" became the greatest show on earth, as magnificent museums arose on the Mall and festival followed festival. Dr. Ripley immediately sensed the convergence of our separate enterprises, and they were soon as one.

And finally, of course, we were lucky in our presidents. Far more than history would have predicted. Once Washington was laid out and working, presidents pretty much lost interest in the place. It was not where they came from nor, yet, where they were going to. There is something somewhere about Franklin D. Roosevelt having decreed that any temporary buildings erected during World War II be designed so as to disintegrate in a quarter century. Yet, forty years later the "tempos" of World War I (in which FDR had worked as assistant secretary of the Navy) were still there on the Mall. The Federal Triangle was unfinished, its largest section a parking lot of "unsurpassed ugliness," as I recall writing. (It is what Arthur J. Goldberg looked out on from his Labor Department Building.) The Avenue, to say again, was disappearing as an urban complex. Worse, the interstate highway system was heading our way: after urban renewal the most devastating influence on American cities in this half of the century. President Eisenhower had lent his name to a proposal for a cultural center, but away from downtown as if it didn't matter all that much.

Then came John F. Kennedy and all that changed. *Pennsylvania Avenue: America's Main Street* tells how in fine detail, and it is not for me to anticipate. I would have to note, however, that like much else, his death brought forth many things he could not achieve in life. One of the last instructions he left before departing for Dallas was that a coffee hour be arranged for the congressional leadership in order to display the model of the Pennsylvania Avenue plan and seek their support. Bill Walton, Charles Horsky, and I were at lunch discussing this on November 22, 1963, when the White House operator called with the news that the president had been shot. We made our way to the White House; the final word came. We left with this task undone.

It took another twenty-five years. Jacqueline Kennedy made it possible. A day or so after the funeral, President Johnson invited Mrs. Kennedy to the Oval Office and asked what he could do for her. She asked for Pennsylvania Avenue. This became known, and made a claim on the Johnson administration. The enterprise acquired official if somewhat skeptical sanction, having been wholly informal under JFK. Richard M. Nixon, somewhat in contrast, was genuinely enthusiastic. He toured the Avenue, displayed the model. Tore down the "tempos." By the time he left office the Pennsylvania Avenue Development Corporation had been established by act of Congress, and there has been no turning back.

On August 21, 1987, the last large piece of the plan was put in place. Terence Golden, a stupendously innovative head of the General Services Administration, had come up with a lease-to-own device whereby the federal government contracted with a developer to lease a newly built building for thirty years at the end of which the government would own it. For this land the intervening rents are at least then market rates, and the result is optimal all round, there being any number of financial institutions that are looking for just such steady and reliable income flows. The land in question used to be that parking lot of "unsurpassed ugliness" between Pennsylvania and Constitution avenues at Fourteenth Street. The new building, with a floor space equivalent to two-thirds that of the Pentagon, would finally bring the major government departments back to federal precincts — the State Department, for example, from sixteen locations in Washington to three — which was a principal proposal of the ad hoc cabinet committee of 1962.

There would be a great atrium, much mixed activity, a board which would include Harry C. McPherson who, as counsel to President Johnson, had saved the plan from extinction in 1964-65. And so at last it seemed at an end: every inch of building line along the 1.1 miles accounted for; everything in place, or soon to be, from the triumphantly restored Willard at one end to the stunning new Canadian Chancery at the other. Or perhaps I should say Nat Owings's reflecting pool, where L'Enfant had looked for a cascade: water of some kind. Make no small plans! I moved the bill in the Senate that August evening and in closing, a bit melodramatic maybe, but, well . . . asked "respectfully to be relieved."

You see, at about midnight of November 22, 1963, I went back to the White House, back to the little warren of rooms where we had awaited word from Dallas that afternoon. Evelyn Lincoln, Kennedy's secretary, had cleared out every scrap of paper from her office, leaving only one of the Bachrach portraits of President Kennedy which he used to sign for, well, I don't know . . . senators, I suppose. I picked it up and went round to the front door of the Oval Office, which was open. I stood at attention: saluted. Steady as she goes. It was a touch I think he might have liked. Anyway, I was young, and I had a quarter century to spare.

*　*　*

That is perhaps too personal. But it is part, I think, of the story, and of a larger point I would wish to make. City planning is a long process, and it requires a measure of commitment that is not likely to be sustained unless there is some grasp of this at the outset. This is especially so in our age. One of the results of the general erosion of the power of political parties and social elites, which could command a measure of acquiescence or deference at the beginning of the century, is that it has become ever more difficult to make large plans and carry them through. In the nineteenth century, Tammany Hall built Central Park in Manhattan. Today any three "community activists" with a lawyer could, and I fear would, prevent Frederick Law Olmsted from even starting. Consider the fate of the Westway, a riverside park that had the potential of equivalent grandeur. There can be no doubt that we were helped in Washington by the absence of anything like organized municipal politics and government in the nation's capital. But the nation cannot settle for stasis. Look at most American cities and ask how much urban development is significant — a Benjamin Franklin Parkway with its flowing acropolis in Philadelphia, Lake Shore Drive in Chicago, the great parks and squares of San Francisco. We get convention centers and hotels. But we don't get any extra *city*. Nothing to be remembered for. "We do not imitate," JFK would quote Pericles addressing the Athenians, "for we are a model to others." But what will be said of us? It may just be that if we read the tale of Pennsylvania Avenue as it deserves to be read, it will give us heart and bring new energies and new men and women to a large calling.

Daniel Patrick Moynihan, Hon. AIA

Pindars Corners, New York
July 4, 1988

Introduction

All nations have a place for common celebration and public sorrow. America's is a broad, shimmering boulevard down the middle of a city that leads a double life, as a pulsing world capital and a sleepy place unto itself. Writing a class paper or sending a letter from Cheyenne, you'd call it Pennsylvania Avenue. There is a seven-mile-long street by that name slashing across Washington, but the heart of it — the symbolic crosswalk of the American democracy — is the "Avenue," a little over a mile's worth of Pennsylvania Avenue connecting the old "President's House" and the "Congress House." It's a dogleg piece of road, dog-eared, too, by a couple of centuries of hooraying and weeping and flooding and any number of rehabilitatings. Nowhere else in the world have presidents and bookmakers, klansmen and civil rights marchers, Yankees off to fight Rebs and doughboys home from the front, slaves in chains and suffragists on Conestoga wagons all passed in life, and more than a few returned in death.

Pennsylvania Avenue has always been a place to be, and to be seen. Millard Fillmore and Franklin Pierce were regular promenaders. Ulysses S. Grant, a merrymaker of a president, showed up one day in Abraham Frank's haberdashery on the Avenue, seeking to get his hat cleaned and blocked; it had been soiled during a White House soiree. According to Abe Frank's grandson, Frank H. Rich, "He conned Grant into buying another one and kept the president's hat as a souvenir."

President Gerald R. Ford — who once joked to an audience of underwriters in California that one of their officers had been a neighbor in Alexandria "until I moved into public housing on Pennsylvania Avenue" — recalled walking the Avenue, as a congressman, with UPI White House correspondent Helen Thomas. "We passed one of those scales that gives you your weight as well as your fortune," Ford recalled, "and all for a penny. Helen said, 'Well, why don't you try it? I might get a scoop.' So I got on the scale, put in a penny, and a card came out that said, 'You are handsome, debonair, sophisticated, a born leader of men, a silver-tongued orator, and some day you will make your mark in history.' Helen leaned over, looked at the card, and said, 'It has your weight wrong, too.'"

One hot, sleepless summer night in August 1963 at the Willard Hotel, where the FBI had routinely wiretapped his room, Martin Luther King, Jr., had put the final touches on his speech to cap off the Poor People's March on Washington the following day. The added language began, "I have a dream." In January 1988, a time capsule containing items from Dr. King's life was embedded in Western Plaza by his widow. That day, the chairman of the Pennsylvania Avenue Development Corporation, Henry A. Berliner, Jr., announced his intention to seek a name change for the city common to Freedom Plaza in Dr. King's memory.

Lady Bird Johnson put in several appearances on the Avenue, contributing flowers for planting all along the boulevard and fussing over tulips in the grassy area that was to become Pershing Park. When she helped dedicate the new Presidential Building at Twelfth Street and the Avenue in 1968, she was greeted with green and blue balloons and huge placards reading "I Like Linden." The celebrants were not poor spellers: They were touting the fragrant new linden trees in front of the building.

Bob Hope showed up on the Avenue whenever the

Top: The Avenue in 1865 featured horse-drawn trolleys on rails. When approaching an incline, the first-string horse received a boost from a "hill horse," which was trained to trot back to its post when the Sisyphean labor was done. The horse in this photo may have been a hill horse — or just some passing nag. For years, the boulevard was full of livestock of many breeds. (Library of Congress)

Bottom: By 1908 the streetcars were electrified by a third rail beneath the pavement. The horses and their phaetons were about to pass into oblivion, but the streetcars withstood the white heat of internal combustion until 1962. (Washingtoniana Division, D.C. Public Library)

USO needed him. Hope had lent his name and part of his collection of USO tour memorabilia to the organization for a museum and fund-raising effort. The USO's local headquarters had occupied a corner of the old Ford Motor Company plant near Fourth Street before it was demolished to make room for the Canadian Chancery.

The Avenue has been called America's most hallowed place and its shabbiest disgrace. It's been pondered and poked fun at, sketched and reconfigured, torn up and torn down more than any other street in the land. Over the years we've bought the freshest fish, drunk the cheapest liquor, caught the quickest cab, and started the longest streetcar ride in Washington along its course. We've changed presidents here, collected great art, tattooed love to Mom, driven sleighs, built a wall of classic buildings, and even lost a Liberty Bell. Not only was "I Have a Dream" written here; so was "Mine Eyes Have Seen the Glory." You'll still find Black Jack and Uncle Billy and Old Ben on the Avenue. The Boss stood here, too, long before Springsteen was born. We've rhapsodized at the view, cheered Lindy and chased Booth, and run cursing from the stench of Tiber Creek. Monumental and minuscule, the Avenue is a compact American morality play, a slice of its good and bad life.

"Pennsylvania Avenue has become an architectural laboratory," said Robert Calhoun Smith, president of Smith-McMahon Architect PC.

Someone once called it a "real-life museum." You've got the geometric challenges of L'Enfant's diagonals and squares, the tricky proposition of framing one of the widest boulevards in the world within Washington's unique height limitations, the difficulty of blending the Federal Triangle's neoclassicism with some of the most modern and individualistic buildings in the city, and an incredible mixture of old and new, large and small, government and private sector. Yet it somehow all works, before the eyes of our nation and thousands of international visitors bringing their own notions of what a great capital should look like. Gone at last are the days when one side of the Avenue or the other was so blighted as to be a national embarrassment. Instead, what a creative place Pennsylvania Avenue has become. The nation can be thankful for the concern that President John F. Kennedy expressed [about the sorry state of the Avenue] following the inauguration parade of 1961.

For parts of seven years, Washington photographer Carol M. Highsmith lugged an old-fashioned 4x5 camera onto and above and around the Avenue to capture an incredible metamorphosis. Her photographs, and those by others here recorded, have thrown open a window on the Avenue, looking down on the march of time.

These are photographs worth studying, for they not only kindle America's collective memories, they also spring some delights. Like the window sign you can just barely spot in an office next to the Grand Army of the Republic Building in 1927: 500 GIRLS WANTED — Light Interesting Work. Or the hill horse. And what is a hill horse? That was the question that one of historian Frederick Gutheim's students asked as she showed him an old, yellowed photograph.

I could see a horse drawing a horsecar on rails, coming up Pennsylvania Avenue and making the corner onto Fifteenth, and another horse, not hitched to anything, standing in the middle of the Avenue. 'That's the hill horse!' my student said. She said the only way tram cars could negotiate the hill at Fifteenth Street was to hook up this extra horsepower, and the two horses then would pull it up the three blocks between Pennsylvania and New York avenues. At that point, before turning west for Georgetown, the conductor would cast loose the hill horse, which was trained to go back to the foot of the hill and wait for the next car to arrive. And that was a hill horse.

For the first time since Pierre-Charles L'Enfant picked his way through the alder bushes, plotting axials and vistas, both sides and all the length of America's great ceremonial way have dignity and charm. The redevelopment, or better, the first real development of the Avenue is not without flaws. Inspiration has danced with drudgery in spots. The Avenue is alive yet not always lively, impressive but not everywhere inviting. But it's finally a place you can take the kids, or Aunt Sally, or the president of Peru, and be proud to show off your Main Street. *Pennsylvania Avenue: America's Main Street* is about to do just that, hill horses and all.

AN AVENUE FIELD GUIDE

From the White House to Freedom Plaza

Some statistical filbert at the District of Columbia planning office once calculated that it takes twenty-six minutes, striding briskly, to cover Pennsylvania Avenue from the Treasury Department terrace at Fifteenth Street to the Capitol steps. Who but a fitness fanatic would, with such a headlong rush, ruin a chance at a more leisurely feast on the sumptuous servings of America's life story?

At least the bureaucrat got the starting line right. The snapshot down the Avenue from Alexander Hamilton's statue is hoary but still a treasure, the distant Capitol steps blurred by snowflakes or ripples of Washington heat but perfectly framed by the looming Old Post Office tower to the right and the delicate turrets of Mathew Brady's onetime studio on the left. A visual grounding is important, for the panoply of important places — a National Hotel here, a Grand Army of the Republic Building there — becomes a jumble without it. The proper way to enjoy the Avenue is a meandering amble, block by block, pausing for dreamlike squints through time at great events, brooding buildings, and the bustling humankind of the American ages. You may still find, as the *National Republic* did in 1870, "a large number of perfect rose-buds (we mean, of course, ladies), the windows of plate glass, those towering crystals that give us brief glimpses as we pass of the fairy halls of fashion within; the gay and varied signs gently swinging in the wind; the spruce-looking men about town; the merry shoe-black, the jocose cab-drivers, the happy house-maids. . . ."

General Sherman's corroded statue in the little park behind the Treasury is worth appreciating before backtracking to the White House. The insets of Uncle Billy's subordinate commanders, the carefully carved and weathered poses of the pillager of Atlanta, seen up close and brushed briefly with the hand, call back the horrors of that terrible Civil War. Before you retrace the inaugural route — in reverse — a double-back is best. A shortcut through East Executive Park beside the White House, with a glance back at one of the city's most pleasing and surprising views of the Washington Monument (ignoring the television trucks), brings you to the east lip of 1600 Pennsylvania Avenue.

Except for a note or two — perhaps something about presidential reviewing stands or the day when sheep grazed on the lawn in a stunt to hype energy conservation — this volume will leave details of that shell-white building, and the lovely Lafayette Park across from it, to ample other works. In each block as you saunter, reflect on what's *Here* and what's *Gone*, how mechanization and history's footprints have tracked L'Enfant's plan, and what time's mists have carried away. Walking the Avenue's imagined median, once possible between Jefferson's Lombardy poplars, the south side is to the right, the north to the left.

Here, in the *1500 block*, after you have posed with a cardboard cutout of the president, you can spot Albert Gallatin, Jefferson's secretary of the treasury, casting a bronzed glare on the Avenue. Is that a satisfied smirk, that Hamilton is out back? Gallatin faces the historic Riggs and American Security bank buildings, which share a facade and, no doubt, a few prominent customers. The Treasury Department's obscure Bureau of Government Financial Operations fills the huge structure to their left. George Washington Riggs, Jr., and a man with another fabled Washington name, William Wilson Corcoran, bought an old Second Bank of the United States branch office on the site, attracted the city elite (Riggs Bank still holds an old Lincoln IOU), and even trundled stacks of cash over to the Treasury via an underground tunnel. *Gone*, on the Financial Ops site, is the Freedman's Savings Bank, created during the Civil War for the use of former slaves and black Union troops. Despite Frederick Douglass's efforts, the bank failed in the 1870s.

Pages 16–17: The Avenue at dusk, looking east toward the Treasury. (Carol M. Highsmith)

Opposite: A standard tourist pose, circa 1948. The Hotel Washington and Occidental Restaurant, Avenue fixtures, are beginning to look frayed. (Washingtoniana Division, D.C. Public Library)

Above: This Lafayette Park kiosk was the departure point for a Herdic cab ride for sight-seeing. One 1884 observer suggested that Peter Herdic's hack service was a fine way to see Washington: "A ride like this will enable a stranger to obtain a general view of the prominent localities in a short time, and serve to fix them in the memory. The route should be taken through the central portions of Pennsylvania Avenue . . . and afterward through the fashionable West End." (Library of Congress)

Right: Major General Marquis Gilbert de Lafayette, represented in a 36-foot-tall bronze memorial in Lafayette Park. At age nineteen, Lafayette volunteered for the Continental army, sailing for the New World on *La Victoire.* Created in 1891 by two sculptors and an architect, the monument depicts America as a woman beckoning to Lafayette for help. Also portrayed are members of the French National Assembly. (Carol M. Highsmith)

20

Left: The White House Easter-egg roll goes back at least as far as 1898, when this portrait was captured. (Frances Benjamin Johnston Collection, Library of Congress)

Below: A 1988 view of the White House featured a freshly striped lawn. According to some accounts, the manse was painted alabaster to hide fire damage inflicted by the British during the War of 1812. (Carol M. Highsmith)

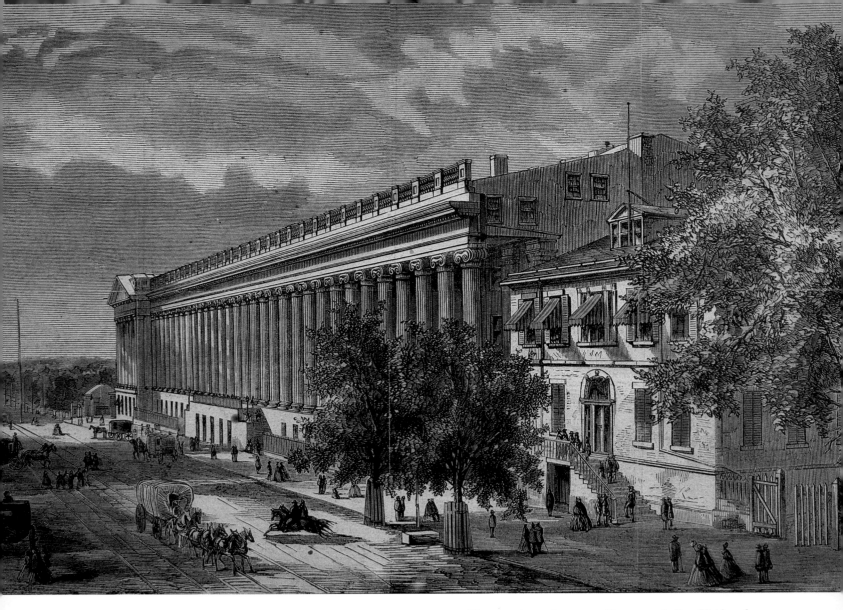

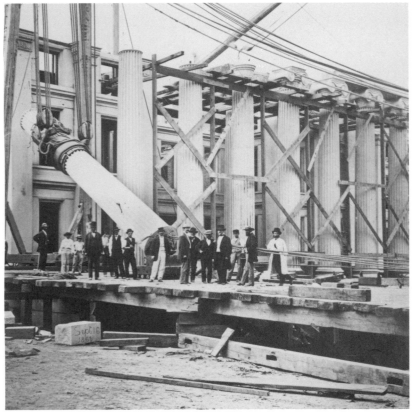

Here, as you turn south around the National Dogleg for a three-block interlude on *Fifteenth Street*, you pass the enormous depth of the Treasury Building and grasp the magnitude of Robert Mills's classic Greek revival building, raised between 1836 and 1851. Its bulk destroyed L'Enfant's wishful vista of the White House from the Capitol, but there is no truth in the old canard that Andy Jackson ordered it so, with a thrust of his cane in a fit of pique against Congress. In fact the legislators chose the site because it lay on affordable government land. *Gone*, to make room for the north wing of the Treasury Building, is the first State Department Building, a modest brick structure intended to be part of a cluster of executive buildings. *Here*, across Fifteenth Street, walking southward and interrupted by G and F streets, are the Perpetual Savings Bank, new Metropolitan Square, and Hotel Washington buildings. More about the hotel as you turn the corner. Metropolitan Square houses the Old Ebbitt Grill, after a fashion, for the actual Ebbitt House was at Fourteenth and F. Historian James M. Goode wrote that the Old Ebbitt boasted massive gas chandeliers "and the city's most prominent coved

ceiling." Another Metropolitan Square tenant, Galt jewelers, traces to an ornate nineteenth-century building, often pictured in inaugural bunting, in the Avenue's 1100 block.

Gone, as well, on the Perpetual site, is the George Washington Hotel, which became simply the Washington Building, home to acclaimed southern cooking in the S&W Cafeteria. And missing is Rhodes Tavern, which stood for 184 years at Fifteenth and F. Rhodes Tavern was the British command post when the redcoats burned the White House, Treasury, and Capitol in 1814. White House architect James Hoban ate there. So did Woodrow Wilson and Harry Houdini and Uncle Joe Cannon. Southern plantation owners met there before crossing the street to the Treasury Building, where they lined up at cashiers' windows to receive compensation for freeing their slaves. Toward the end a Washington businessman offered to buy and move the tiny tavern, but, in September 1984, minutes after a court of appeals turned down a citizens' group entreaty, bulldozers tore Rhodes Tavern into a memory. Protestors and passersby alike scooped up bricks as souvenirs.

Opposite top: An 1845 woodcut shows not only the sweep of Treasury, but also the modest State Department edifice, long torn down. There's no truth to the myth that Andrew Jackson dropped Treasury's bulk right into the Avenue's midst out of pure churlishness. Congressional penury is a more accurate explanation. (Kiplinger Collection)

Opposite bottom: Workers hoisting one of seventy-four granite columns imported by sailing ship from Maine to install on the Treasury edifice in 1861. Thirteen teams of horses and oxen were needed to pull each column through city streets. Though started under Andrew Jackson, the building was not finished until 1869. (National Archives)

Above: Rhodes Tavern in 1801, its initial year on the section of Fifteenth Street connecting the Pennsylvania Avenue inaugural route. The brick building was the British command post when the redcoats burned the White House, Treasury, and Capitol in 1814. (Kiplinger Collection)

Top: In 1875, the upper Avenue looked almost like a scene from Bath, England, with this collection of Federal-style row houses grouped near a crescent. This row gave way to the liveliness of the Oxford Hotel and Poli's, where some recall Blackstone the Magician skimming playing cards into the seats. (James M. Goode Collection, Library of Congress) *Bottom:* In 1925, the buildings at Fifteenth and Pennsylvania formed a lively mix. From left: The Grand Army of the Republic Building, Poli's Theater — said to be as ugly outside as it was exquisite within — and the Oxford Hotel. Within years all were swept away in the enthusiasm for building an extension of the Commerce Department as a cog in the Federal Triangle. The bricks-and-mortar plan never came to pass, but bulrushes and ice skaters did. Today the site is home to Pershing Park. (Columbia Historical Society)

Opposite: Pershing Park, designed by architect M. Paul Friedberg as a place for contemplation. Landscape architects lined it with American and Chinese grasses and planted water lilies and lotuses in the pond. The result: A family of mallards became the first live-ins on the refreshed Avenue. (Carol M. Highsmith)

Turning onto the *1400 block* of the Avenue proper, you arrive at its trickiest part. *Here*, in the center of the broad boulevard, is the astonishingly serene Pershing Park, a creation of the Pennsylvania Avenue Development Corporation. Its greenery screens a dozen charms, from the old-stone vault and water cascade (which is not really old but was created to stow the Zamboni ice-making machine for the park's skating rink) to the granite tableau recalling Black Jack Pershing and the Great War battles of the western front. *Gone*, and hard to visualize, is a string of "Treasury Square" row houses — right where the park now lies. They, and the ponderous GAR building, whose Romanesque tower hovered in turn-of-the-century views, once lined the south side of a much narrower Avenue. The Oxford Hotel and Poli's Theater (originally an opera house, then a burlesque) were there, too. Washington editor Austin Kiplinger remembered sitting, enthralled, at Poli's, watching Blackstone the Magician sail cards into the balcony.

Here on today's south side stands the Department of Commerce Building, the first structure completed in the massive Federal Triangle, a creation of the depression days. In its great hall before World War II, inventors were required not just to show plans but also to demonstrate their sometimes bizarre contraptions. Like other Federal Triangle buildings, Commerce replaced a jumble of stores and industrial shops. Triangle plans originally called for extending the Commerce Building northward. Poli's and adjacent structures were demolished accordingly. But when money ran out in the depression's swoon, the area reverted to green space. The tuliped lawn that preceded Pershing Park was one of the Avenue's few visual emollients during its postwar decline. *Here*, on the Avenue's north side, are the Hotel Washington (opened in 1917 and now the city's oldest continuously operating hotel) and the New Willard. The Washington rose on the site of the old Corcoran Office Building, whose awninged corner is seen in many vintage photos; parades of all descriptions headed for home around that turn. The Willard will get its own treatment later. *Gone*, in what is now the courtyard and Occidental Restaurant between the two hotels, are a hideous, three-level parking garage, the original and fashionable Occidental, and a skinny, eight-story Occidental Hotel that was separate from the restaurant. Where the eating house, with its walls of photographs of the high and the mighty — and its roast beef and rum buns — was the posh politicos' hangout in its heyday, the hotel became a haven of lobbying of the supine sort.

From Freedom Plaza to Market Square

You can't find your way around the Avenue's *1300 block* without an alphabet. Freedom Plaza (née Western Plaza, once a barren traffic island and almost part of a grandiose planned National Square) was home to two memorable sculptures. A statue of Alexander "Boss" Shepherd stood here until the Pennsylvania Avenue Development Corporation built Western Plaza; Boss went off to storage on the grounds of the city's Blue Plains waste-disposal facility, where he lay on a stack of tires for eight years until he was given a new pedestal on

Shepherd Parkway in southwest Washington. The other piece was a replica of the Liberty Bell, cast in Philadelphia and presented to the District of Columbia government as part of a 1950 national savings-bond drive. The bell turned up missing in the dust of PADC street renovation. PADC says it parked it in a fenced-in spot at John Marshall Park; the District heard it went to some youth group. Philip Ogilvie, archivist for the District, even nosed around the grounds of the Campfire Girls of America, hunting unsuccessfully for the bell. Surviving the purge of Western Plaza monuments is the equestrian statue of the revolutionary war patriot, Polish General Casimir Pulaski. *Here* on the south side stands city hall, the intricate District Building, ringed by twenty-eight allegorical statues. Completed on more than twenty-five hundred pilings in soupy tidal soil in 1908, the District Building was constructed at a time when the city was run by three commissioners; thus, there are three plush corner offices rather than one, each with a fireplace. Renovations begun in 1988 finally addressed the building's unintended adornments, replacing with a central system the hundreds of window air conditioners that stuck through building windows. *Gone* in the space now occupied by a parking lot are three historic buildings: the Prescott House Hotel, which doubled as a political prison; the brownstone renaissance revival Southern Railway Building; and a nondescript U.S. Coast Guard Building that was removed in the 1970s, in hopes of creating a verdant plaza. Instead, more cars gobbled the space.

Here, on the north side, along what was once called E Street, is the first result of PADC's "mixed-use" development, the strip containing the J. W. Marriott Hotel, The Shops at National Place arcade, and the restored National Theatre. Although not part of the overall project, the twelve-story American Cities office building at 1301 Pennsylvania Avenue was also built by one of National Place's developers, Quadrangle Development Corporation. *Gone*, at Pennsylvania Avenue and Fourteenth Street, once Washington's busiest intersection, are street cops who maneuvered hand-operated semaphore signals. A memory, too, are the murky Munsey office building and the Washington Post Building, and, around the corner on Fourteenth Street, an entire Newspaper Row.

Opposite: Avenue planners banished the likeness of Boss Shepherd, one of the Avenue's great civilizers. But not this statue of Casimir Pulaski, who preferred his Polish marshal's uniform to that of the Continental army. The revolutionary war hero provides a striking foreground for the Old Post Office. (Carol M. Highsmith)

Above: Traffic cops operated manual signals on the Avenue from the early days of auto traffic until about 1925. The auto in this 1915 photo, taken at Fourteenth Street, is a Haynes. (Harris & Ewing Photos, Library of Congress)

Here, looking over Freedom Plaza in the *1200 block,* is developer Richard S. Cohen's Pennsylvania Building at 1275 Pennsylvania Avenue — a remake of a 1950s-drab predecessor. Old photographs show a prominent attraction on the site: Warwick's Billiard Parlors, one of the fanciest pool halls in the East. Next to the Pennsylvania Building, and angling inward down the Avenue, is Cabot, Cabot and Forbes's sleek 1201 Pennsylvania Avenue Building. *Gone,* on the same north side, are the offices (but never the brewery) of the Christian Heurich Brewing Company and an old service station. *Here,* on the south side, is the facade of another sweeping Federal Triangle building, the Ariel Rios Building, named for a federal agent killed by narcotics dealers. Once called the New Post Office, and still a substation, it houses the Bureau of Alcohol, Tobacco and Firearms. *Gone* to make room for Rios is a popular tavern called the One-Two-Three-Four at . . . 1234 Pennsylvania!

Above: This Civil War–era view depicts the Newspaper Row of Washington bureaus for out-of-town papers. Most eventually consolidated under the single roof of the National Press Club. William McKinley lived at the Ebbitt House while he was a member of Congress from 1876 to 1890. (Brown Brothers, New York City)

Left: The Washington Post Building in 1917. Note at right Shoomaker's saloon, server of "perpendicular" drinks. (Library of Congress)

Right: The proximity of the Washington Post and Evening Star buildings helped spawn Newspaper Row near Fourteenth Street. In 1890, several publications ganged up behind this prenouveau facade. (Proctor Collection)

Left: These 1890s billiards players were a far cry from the tattooed poolroom denizens of today. The sport was for the genteel set. None of Washington's game rooms was more grandly burnished than Warwick's Billiard Parlor, with not even a cuspidor in sight. (James M. Goode Collection, Library of Congress)

Below: The sleek 1201 Pennsylvania has been a tremendous success with its office tenants. One law firm actually led in a parade when it took occupancy. But its restaurants have failed, putting a slight damper on Avenue nightlife. (Carol M. Highsmith)

You arrive next at the *1100 block*, one of the Avenue's most historic sectors. *Here*, on the north side, are the 1964 Presidential office building, housing a bank and savings and loan, and the 1898 Evening Star Building, which kept its facade and lost its innards in a renovation. The *Star* was once published across the Avenue when Eleventh Street cut through. Both that building and the street were casualties when the Romanesque Post Office Building, now gnarled enough to be called the *Old* Post Office, rose in 1899. *Gone* on the north side is the hulking, intricately inlaid, white-brick Raleigh Hotel, a Washington fixture from 1898 to 1964. "Through the years the Raleigh has lost its grandeur," James Goode quotes the hotel's last manager, "but never its dignity." Two predecessor buildings on the Raleigh site, the Kirkwood Hotel and the Shepherd Centennial Building, are often seen, bedecked, in early inaugural prints and photos. As Richard M. Lee tells it in *Mr. Lincoln's City*, one of John Wilkes Booth's fellow conspirators, George Atzerodt, had taken a room directly above Vice President Andrew Johnson's room at the Kirkwood. "He was supposed to knock at Johnson's door at about the same moment that Booth was to shoot Mr. Lincoln. . . . Atzerodt lost his nerve, took to drinking and ran away without making an attempt. As a member of the conspiracy, he was later hanged anyway." Johnson was sworn in as president at the Kirkwood the next day. The 1889 statue of Benjamin Franklin ("Philosopher — Printer — Philanthropist — Patriot"), at the northwest corner of the Old Post Office, once stood on a traffic island on the Avenue's north side.

Top: Vice President Andrew Johnson became known as a habitué of the Kirkwood Hotel, which almost led to his demise by assassination. A conspirator of John Wilkes Booth stalked Johnson there, but lost his nerve. He was caught and hanged. (Columbia Historical Society)

Middle: The Boss himself, Governor Alexander Robey Shepherd, built this office building in 1876, the nation's hundredth anniversary. It lasted thirty-five years, supplanted by the Raleigh Hotel. (Columbia Historical Society)

Bottom: Designed by Willard architect Henry Janeway Hardenbergh, the Raleigh Hotel at Twelfth Street didn't stick around long enough to attract a preservationist following. Said its last manager, "The Raleigh has lost its grandeur, but never its dignity." (James M. Goode Collection, Library of Congress)

Here on the stubby *1000 block's* north side, and set back behind a triple row of trees, is Canadian developer Cadillac-Fairview's 1001 Pennsylvania Avenue office building, whose concourses converge on a remarkable rotunda lobby. For the filming of the movie *Broadcast News*, director James Brooks turned 1001 Penn into a virtual Hollywood set for six months in 1987. Twentieth Century-Fox leased twelve thousand square feet on the second floor from Cadillac-Fairview's successor, Prentiss Properties, covered floor-to-ceiling windows with a fake wall, and built a simulated twenty-five-year-old television studio — preserving, through smaller windows, the view across the Avenue to the Old Post Office and the Internal Revenue Service Building. On film, actors Jack Nicholson and William Hurt popped into and out of lobby elevators; building tenants who wished to did likewise as extras. Hollywood notables hobnobbed at Avenue sandwich shops and coffee wagons.

Across Pennsylvania Avenue, past the Old Post Office's sidewalk cafe, stands the facade of another Federal Triangle component, the Internal Revenue Service Building. Inspired by the design of the Somerset House on the Strand in London, headquarters of the British Inland Revenue Office, the IRS Building saves its principal entrance for Constitution Avenue to the rear. *Gone*, on the north side are nondescript Victorian office buildings, whose ground floors housed shops like "Thomas Booth, Umbrella Maker" in the nineteenth century and Souvenir World in the twentieth. *Gone* on the south side are Harvey's oyster house, the New Lyceum vaudeville house, and Espey's hardware store.

Above: This grand cruciform at 1001 Pennsylvania attracted the eye of the film producers for *Broadcast News.* They shot much of the 1987 comedy in the structure, a compendium of the block's historic facades melded to new innards. The action sent William Hurt and Jack Nicholson scurrying up and down the building's elevators. Tenants served as extras. The antique-looking "brass" clock is actually new precast aluminum made in Salt Lake City from a design by Graham Davidson of Washington, D.C., architects Hartman-Cox. (Carol M. Highsmith)

Right: A 1909 facade was preserved as part of 1001 Pennsylvania. These "facadism" projects were typical of PADC's work, which favored compromise solutions over pure preservation. But PADC came a long way from its urban-renewal roots of the early 1970s, when the Willard Hotel was slated for demolition. (Carol M. Highsmith)

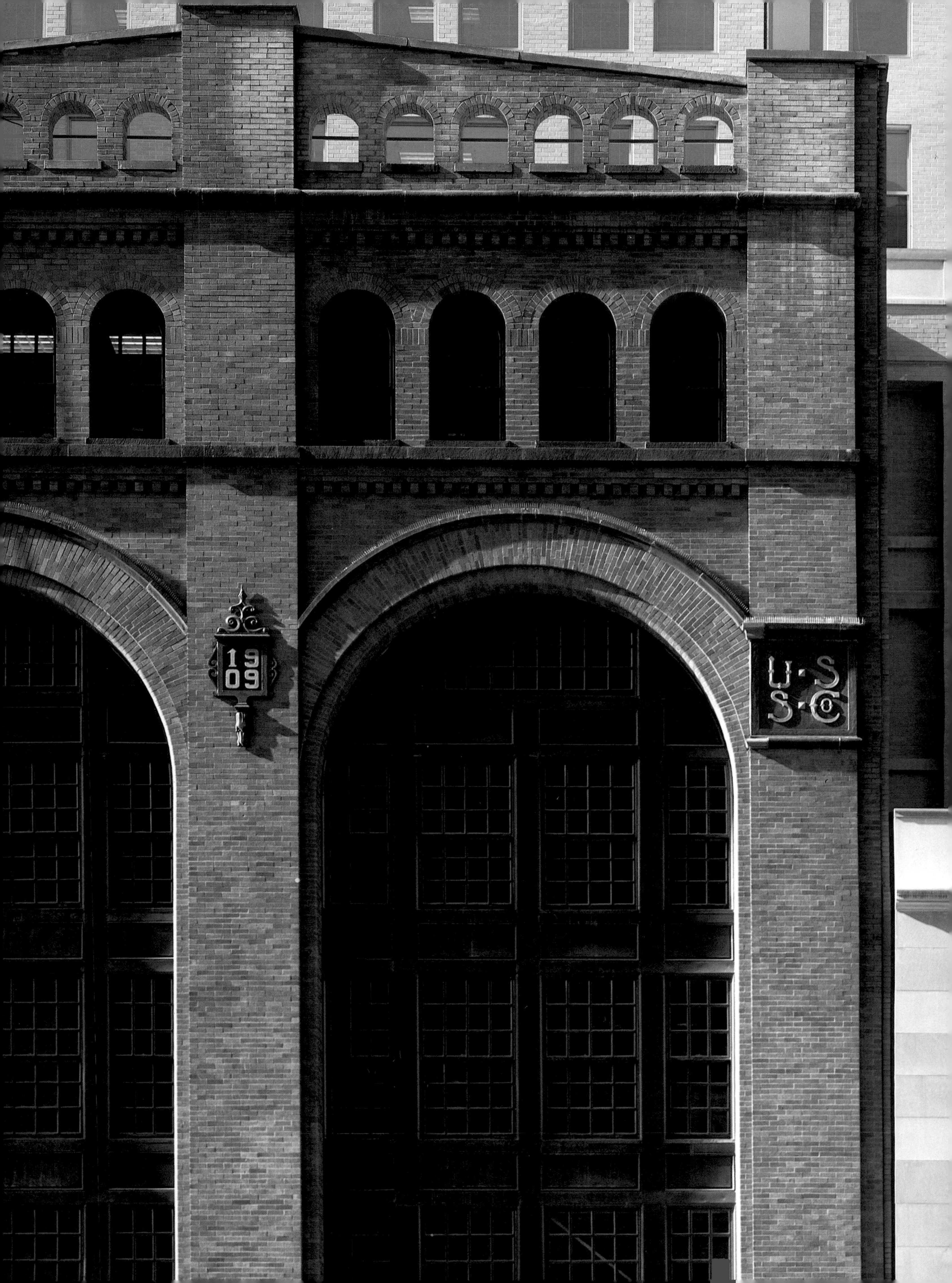
1909
U·S
S·Co

Left: In 1867, the hot book for sale at French & Richardson Bookstore was *Nicholas Nickleby*, Dickens's novel of 1839. The building survived until 1963, when it was razed to make way for the FBI Building (James M. Goode Collection, Library of Congress)

Above: Finery and frippery were the order of the day in 1889, when this shot was taken in the Tenth Street banking area. It wasn't all sobriety in the financial district, however; note the Swedish Movements and Massage enticement on Vernon Row. Apparently you could stop for more than a loan. (Library of Congress)

The *900 block* is consumed, on the north side, by the J. Edgar Hoover FBI Building, which wiped out a block of D Street. More about this magnet of controversy elsewhere. *Here*, on the south, is another federal clone, the Department of Justice. *Gone*, on the north: Metzerott Hall, a popular music store whose cast-iron facade fell into Pennsylvania Avenue in 1894, killing a clerk. A famous bookstore, French & Richardson, occupied the block, as did the second site of the Boston Dry Goods Store, a predecessor of Woodward & Lothrop department store. *Gone*, on the south side, is a portion of the Hay Market, a scraggly, outdoor neighbor of the larger Center Market to the east. In the midst of the market's queues of produce wagons stood Canterbury's, a rowdy music hall, and, during the Civil War, the Union army's central guardhouse.

To the Capitol

ennsylvania Avenue's north-side *800* and *700 blocks* (Eighth Street does not penetrate the south side) cradle the nascent Market Square and Navy Memorial projects. The simple, bronze *Lone Sailor* statue stands on a giant stone disc, inscribed with a world map. He depicts a bluejacket who, the navy says, is "a senior second class petty officer who is fast becoming a seagoing veteran. He has done it all — fired his weapons in a dozen wars, weighed anchor from a thousand ports, tracked supplies, doused fires, repelled boarders, typed in quadruplicate, and mess-cooked, too." Colonnaded towers of office, retail, and residential space, developed by Avenue Associates Limited Partnership, form a semicircle around the memorial. These towers are among the PADC's later development pieces. Filling out the block is the figure of General Winfield Hancock, whose eyes avoid both the navy man and the yawning entrance to the Archives Metro subway station. *Here*, to the south, is the National Archives Building, squared to preserve L'Enfant's notion of a widened midpoint respite in the Avenue. Note the two stone neoclassic statues, the male Roman scholar (Study the Past) and a female representing the future (What is Past is Prologue).

Anyone who pondered the contribution to American history of Franklin Delano Roosevelt might expect to find, somewhere in Washington, a hefty monument to the thirty-second president, who served four terms. A monument is there, all right, in a triangular strip of grass before the Archives Building. But it's anything but colossal. Roosevelt's friend, Felix Frankfurter, was summoned to the president's office one day in 1941. FDR informed the Supreme Court justice, "I am likely to shuffle off long before you kick the bucket," as Frankfurter recalled the conversation. "If they are to put up any memorial to me, I should like it to be placed in the center of that green plot in front of the Archives Building. I should like it to consist of a block about the size of this [putting his hand on his desk]." And so was it done. A simple granite block, etched In Memory of FRANKLIN DELANO ROOSEVELT, 1882-1945, was dedicated on the Avenue in 1965.

Opposite: Detail of National Archives, the repository that grew where vendors of Center Market once sold the freshest fish in town. (Carol M. Highsmith)

Above: General Winfield Scott Hancock, a Civil War hero honored in this 1896 bronze statue, appears ready to grab the Sears House finial as a lance to match his charger. (Carol M. Highsmith)

Center Market straddled Seventh Street to Ninth, where it blocked L'Enfant's intended view of a never-built pantheon. On the other hand, wrote David Ballie Warden in 1816, Avenue markets provided "two of the luxuries of life, pine-apples and ice." (James M. Goode Collection, Library of Congress)

Gone from that south-side superblock is the old Center Market, the city's one-stop shopping center for more than 150 years. The long, brick indoor pavilion, constructed in 1872, was razed for Federal Triangle construction in 1931. For a time, the market was run by the U.S. Department of Agriculture itself. Demolished, too, was a resplendent beaux-arts comfort station facing Seventh Street in front of the market. *Gone* along Market Space on the north side are the old Avenue House Hotel; the Sleep Center, which marked forty years in 1977; Kann's department store; and a variety of smaller shops (Carter's Dry Goods, W. B. Moses furniture and carpet shop, Ruppert's cigar store). Kann's called its location "Kann's Busy Corner," and Seventh and the Avenue was indeed, for a century, the vortex of Washington commerce.

The *600 block* marks the apex of the Federal Triangle, and the smallest of its structures, the Federal Trade Commission Building. Guarded by Michael Lantz's 1942 statue of *Man Controlling Trade* (trade is a horse), the building is imaginatively known as the Apex Building. Its two art deco aluminum doors facing the Avenue feature ships and planes and other mechanical slaves of commerce. *Here*, on the north side, is another triangular block, snipping into D Street and Indiana Avenue. A pleasant corner plaza is home to the GAR statue, which salutes Charity, Fraternity, and Dr. Benjamin F. Stephenson, the GAR's founder. Standing impishly nearby is the Cogswell Temperance Fountain. Two frolicking dolphins surround the fountain, and a water crane stretches its neck above. At one time it featured a device that forced water over a block of ice, a salubrious alternative to the bane of San Francisco dentist Henry Cogswell's society: Demon Rum. *Here*, too, on the north side is another, private-sector version of an Apex Building. Once it housed Apex Liquors, a discount emporium that would have set Dr. Cogswell's teeth to gnashing. A century ago, the building held Gilman's Drugs and Brady's photo studio. The lavishly remodeled building, today known as Sears House, is home to the retail giant's government affairs office. A memory, too, are the Avenue Billiard Parlor and the fabled Brown's Indian Queen (later Metropolitan) Hotel, named for a swinging sign that bore a likeness of Pocahontas. A vestige of another era does remain on the block's northeast corner: the old Atlantic Coast Line [Railroad] Building, which has become part of the 601 Pennsylvania Avenue office and retail project. *Gone* on the south side is a succession of shops, private homes, and boardinghouses.

Top: The Temperance Fountain and its abstaining crane were reinstated on a refurbished Indiana Plaza in 1987. (Carol M. Highsmith)

Bottom: The beaux-arts style of this 1910 comfort station may have architecturally outshone the facility it served: Center Market. Both were torn down for Federal Triangle construction. (Library of Congress)

Top: The National Hotel was one of Andy Jackson's favorite haunts. Here festered the mysterious National Hotel sickness, which felled several guests during the 1857 inauguration of James Buchanan. The wreckers didn't arrive until 1942. Note the rutted streets. The Avenue had proved impervious to macadamizing efforts of the 1830s. (Library of Congress)

Bottom: The Victorianized Hotel Fritz Reuter, which featured a German restaurant and wine cellar, stood near Fourth Street in 1890. (James M. Goode Collection, Library of Congress)

Opposite: The National Gallery East Building replaced a tennis court and 120 climbing red-rose bushes. It was designed to complement the Avenue by I. M. Pei, a recipient of the Gold Medal from the American Institute of Architects. (Carol M. Highsmith)

The Avenue has little to recommend it on the south side of the *500 block*. A tiny park, honoring National Gallery of Art patron Andrew W. Mellon, fills the triangle formed where Constitution Avenue slashes across Pennsylvania. Only a small corner of the mighty gallery faces the Avenue here. Opened in 1941, the National Gallery was the largest gift ever presented by a private citizen to any government. The Gallery replaced the seventy-year-old headquarters building of the American Colonization Society, which helped freed blacks find what was touted as an African workers' paradise. The West African colonies of "Liberia" and "Maryland" would eventually merge into the Liberian democracy. *Here*, too, and eminently passable next to the Canadians' new building on the north side, is a 1960s boxy structure, the D.C. Employment Security Building, due for replacement by PADC. Mrs. Peyton's heralded boardinghouse once occupied the chancery site; the prominent National Hotel, a favorite hostelry of southern gentlemen, the Employment Security location. Henry Clay died at the National, Andrew Jackson walked from it to his swearing-in ceremony, and Booth would think of staying nowhere else when he was in town. A Ford Motor Company assembly plant, remodeled to house the local USO and Metropolitan Police offices, and a second nondescript government office building fell to build the Canadian Chancery. Henry Ford unveiled the new Model A at the auto plant in 1927. *Gone* on the south side is John C. Howard's Livery Stable, where Booth bought a horse in his dash to escape Lincoln's avengers.

National Gallery Director J. Carter Brown summed up architect I. M. Pei's challenge in designing a new East Building on the south side of another megablock, *300 to 500* Pennsylvania Avenue:

None of the speculative architects who said they'd like the job ever had a facade that fronted Pennsylvania Avenue. They were thinking entirely of the geometry of the Mall. The problem is that this trapezoidal site doesn't allow a facade to match the facade of the National Gallery, because the center of the site is south of there. . . . The scale is such that it wouldn't really stand up to the main building. My father warned me when we were doing the project that you don't want it to look as if the National Gallery had a pup. . . . You had this spaghetti of intersecting streets and nothing to terminate the march of buildings along the Mall or to shore up the march of buildings along Pennsylvania. And so it was Pei's vision to devise a building that would do both things. . . . From a Pennsylvania Avenue point of view it frames the Capitol and does right all the way back up to the Treasury. So I think from an urban-design point of view it really is the start of the Pennsylvania Avenue experience.

Gone to build the East Building are a long-standing tennis court and 120 climbing red-rose bushes planted on the court fence as part of Lady Bird Johnson's beautification blitz. Much earlier, row-shops and a Chinese-owned funeral home filled the block. *Here* on the north side is John Marshall Park, a PADC creation from the closed former entrance to the city's municipal complex. Four-and-one-half Street through the area became a series of stairwayed city mesas, complete with Marshall statue and pondering chess players. A U.S. courthouse and the statue to General George G. Meade, the victor at Gettysburg, surrounded by figures in various stages of undress, complete the northside block.

Gone from the courthouse site is Washington's original Chinatown. A Chinese import-export

shop, a restaurant, and an herb shop were part of it before Chinatown moved to H Street in advance of courthouse construction. Harrison Lee, a retired CIA employee who grew up on the Avenue's Chinatown strip, said he remembered "banana carts, ice trucks, the smell of fresh bread baking and coffee grinding," and the cordial relations with Greek and Italian merchants who also crowded the east end of the Avenue. As for the looming sight of the U.S. Capitol three blocks away, "It didn't make much of an impression until we studied U.S. history." Well before Chinatown, the Saint Charles Hotel, facing Third at Penn, had incorporated four columns from the Capitol after its burning by the British; the Saint Charles's basement slave pens were a notorious feature of the hotel. Later it became the favorite hotel of delegations of American Indians.

Left: By 1946 autos were rolling down the Avenue in record numbers. But that doesn't mean that a couple of pairs of well-turned legs couldn't stop traffic, as they did on this occasion at John Marshall Place. (Washingtoniana Division, D.C. Public Library)

Right: At 464 Pennsylvania, Jackson Hall was raised in 1845 for large parties such as Zachary Taylor's inaugural ball. The ballroom was later converted to a printshop for the *Congressional Globe,* a forerunner of the *Congressional Record.* (National Archives)

Below: The New Capital (née Saint Charles) Hotel incorporated four columns salvaged from the U.S. Capitol after its torching by the British. Its basement slave pens were notorious. Later it became a favorite convention hotel for delegations of American Indians. The building endured from 1816 to 1920. (James M. Goode Collection, Library of Congress)

Left: The Peace Monument, an 1877 ode to the navy dead of the Civil War. It was carved in Rome by Franklin Simmons. The allegorical figures atop the 40-foot-tall monument represent America crying on History's shoulder. (Carol M. Highsmith)

Right: Semi-nude Lieutenant General George Washington overlooked the Avenue processional route from a U.S. Capitol aerie on the West Front from 1841 until the Civil War, when this sculpture by Horatio Greenough was moved to the East Front. Now it's set in a Smithsonian museum. (Frances Benjamin Johnston Collection, Library of Congress)

Below right: Walt Whitman stayed at the Hotel Brunswick, a boarding-house next to Tiber Creek. Whitman came to Washington during the Civil War to attend to the wounded. He would dispense cigars, postage stamps, and conversation on daily rounds through hospitals. His friend, the naturalist John Burroughs, wrote: "As he took his way toward the door, you could hear the voices of many a stricken hero calling, 'Walt, Walt, Walt! Come again! Come again!' " (Columbia Historical Society; Whitman photo by Mathew Brady, National Portrait Gallery)

The stolid Frances Perkins Labor Building sits astride Third Street just north of the Avenue (closer, technically, to Constitution Avenue, which has crossed Pennsylvania on its own route toward the Capitol), above a massive underground freeway that was supposed to be part of a loop through the city, on its blissful way to the Capital Beltway. Citizens' groups stopped the expressway at New York Avenue. In the Perkins Building's courtyard is an abstract glob of iron called *SHE*, presumably not inspired by Mrs. Perkins. *Gone* from the site is the old Esso Building, which James Goode recalled as "a delightful beaux-arts building that could have been a wonderful House office building."

The *100* and *200* blocks have been denuded of structures, save for the Capitol Reflecting Pool, opened in 1971, and, in the traffic circle beneath the Capitol's west front, the Peace Monument, built in 1877 to honor the navy's Civil War dead. *Gone* from both blocks are souvenir shops, tour-bus depots, and boardinghouses like the old Hotel Brunswick. Poet Walt Whitman wrote his mother that one of the rooming houses "is a miserable place — very bad air." No wonder; about half a block away flowed Tiber Creek, the city's favorite sewer.

Twenty-six minutes indeed! It takes as long to savor *each block* of Pennsylvania Avenue, particularly with stops for those squints through time.

45

Above: Capitol newsboys, circa 1910.
(Lewis Hine photo, collection of John
C. DePrez, Jr.)

Right: The Capitol at sunrise.
(Carol M. Highsmith)

46

WHAT'S PAST IS PROLOGUE

Slop on the Avenue

Pierre-Charles L'Enfant did not conjure up a lofty world capital out of primeval ooze, though the spot was plenty swampy. Twenty plantations and two modest tobacco wharves — Hamburg on the Potomac and Carrolsburg on the Eastern Branch — had traded, even raising eyebrows in palmy Georgetown and Alexandria, for twenty years before the mercurial French planner and President Washington tramped the territory together. Washington fiddled a bit with the young major's geometry, ordering the President's House a few hundred yards from where L'Enfant had intended it. The president had gotten his way, as he did with everything, in selecting the Potomac basin as the capital in the first place, influenced by his own prosperity at nearby Mount Vernon and by the new capital's likely ease of access up the Potomac to Cumberland and the West. In solitary reconnaissance later, Major L'Enfant took special note of the area's topography. A long ridge overlooked the river, and at its highest point, Jenkins' Hill, he drew the site for the nation's new Congress House. Washington had already picked a place for the President's House, a little more than a mile away. So L'Enfant's baroque Plan of the City in 1791 began with a broad avenue, interrupted by three large spaces, which he saw as a great processional route between the seats of power.

1791

Onto his sketch L'Enfant imposed a minor order, the traditional grid of lettered and numbered streets compelled by the city commissioners, as well as his own higher one, with a goosefoot arrangement of avenues fanning from population buds that he foresaw throughout this envisioned ten-mile-square city to be carved from the hills and woods. On a line due west from the Congress House, he drew his Mall — he called it a "vast esplanade" — for embassies, the city's grandest homes, and, he wrote Secretary of State Thomas Jefferson, "all such sort of places as may be attractive to the learned and afford diversion to the idle." Running straight along the Mall at a spot due south of the President's House, he imagined an equestrian statue to honor Washington, his patron. Midway down a grand canal, carved from Tiber Creek just below his great axial avenue, he placed a turning basin, around which a commercial center was sure to grow. A little above one of this avenue's grand spaces, he saw a pantheon, a place to honor and bury the nation's dead. L'Enfant was thinking big.

Despite his slashing radials, L'Enfant's was not a linear plan. Rather than a Main Street America notion of growth beginning thinly along a boulevard and bulking out from it on both sides, he saw distinct enclaves scattered about town. Someday, perhaps a hundred years hence, the spaces between these nodes might coalesce. Vistas along the avenues were symbolic in their own right. What would soon be christened Pennsylvania Avenue was, more than anything, the shortest distance between the capital's two greatest points. "L'Enfant could not have visualized the automobile, or even the train," noted Seattle architect Paul Thiry, who drew one of many wholesale redesigns of the Avenue in the 1960s. "Streets that crossed the Avenue at thirty- and sixty-degree angles would be hard for them to negotiate, but to the planner in slower times, times of carriages and promenading, distant sight lines were imperative."

Washington architect Sibley Jennings has argued that if the temperamental Frenchman had the gleam of a "Grand Avenue," it was his great Mall. Jennings deduces that it was a combination of myth, surveyor Andrew Ellicott's *interpretation* of L'Enfant's plan — and perhaps intrigue, antipapism, and even envy by Jefferson of L'Enfant's bond to Washington — that led to a distortion of the

Lat. Capitol,.... 38: 53, N.
Long.............0: 0.

GEORGE TOWN

PLAN
of the CITY of
Washington
in the Territory of Columbia,
ceded by the States of
VIRGINIA and MARYLAND
to the
United States of America,
and by them established as the
SEAT of their GOVERNMENT,
after the Year
MDCCC.

Engraved by Thackara & Vallance Philad.ᵃ 1792.

PART OF VIRGINIA WITHIN THE TERRITORY OF COLUMBIA.

President's House

Capitol

P O T O M A K   R I V E R

E A S T E R N   B R A N C H

PART OF MARYLAND WITHIN THE TERRITORY OF COLUMBIA.

OBSERVATIONS
explanatory of the
Plan.

THE positions for the different Edifices, and for the several Squares or Areas of different shapes, as they are laid down, were first determined on the most advantageous ground, commanding the most extensive prospects, and the better susceptible of such improvements, as either use or ornament may hereafter call for.

LINES or Avenues of direct communication have been devised, to connect the separate and most distant objects with the principal, and to preserve through the whole a reciprocity of sight at the same time. Attention has been paid to the passing of these leading Avenues over the most favorable ground for prospect and convenience.

NORTH and South lines intersected by others running due East and West, make the distribution of the City into Streets, Squares, &c. and these lines have been so combined as to meet at certain given points with those divergent Avenues, so as to form on the Spaces first determined, the different Squares or Areas.

SCALE OF POLES.

Breadth of the Streets.

THE grand Avenues, and such Streets as lead immediately to public places, are from 130 to 160 feet wide, and may be conveniently divided into foot ways, walks of trees, and a carriage way. The other Streets are from 90 to 110 feet wide.

IN order to execute this plan, Mr. ELLICOTT drew a true Meridional line by celestial observation, which passes through the Area intended for the Capitol; this line he crossed by another due East and West, which passes through the same Area. These lines were accurately measured, and made the basis on which the whole plan was executed. He ran all the lines by a Transit Instrument, and determined the Acute Angles by actual measurement, and left nothing to the uncertainty of the Compass.

Pages 48–49: Pennsylvania Avenue stands out like a great escarpment in this 1880 print by Currier & Ives. (Kiplinger Collection)

Opposite: L'Enfant, shown here giving George Washington a tour of his new capital in 1791, called Jenkins' Hill "a pedestal waiting for a monument." His boulevard leading to the president's "palace" would have to be cut through subtropical growth. (Architect of the Capitol)

Above: After L'Enfant's stormy departure, Major Andrew Ellicott put his name on the plan for the new capital. This 1792 map shows the original, unimpeded vista between the White House and the Capitol. (National Park Service)

tormented Frenchman's dream. But it was assuredly Pennsylvania Avenue about which Washington himself wrote, in his report accompanying L'Enfant's plan. "The Grand Avenue connecting both the palace and the federal house will be most magnificent & most convenient," he jotted, and he ordered that it "be built up at once."

So obviously was Pennsylvania Avenue first among equals that L'Enfant extended the artery clear to Georgetown to the west and to the Potomac's Eastern Branch, or Anacostia River, on the east. The new road was surveyed and the ground grubbed over, and an overseer ordered to give it "a breadth two perches done in the middle." America's Main Street was born with that command, on April 14, 1792. So slowly did work proceed, though, that four years later, the commissioners were writing to inform landowner Daniel Burnes that they could not be held responsible for ruining his crops if he continued to sow seeds in ground intended for its course.

51

Why *Pennsylvania* Avenue? No correspondent ever thought to ask L'Enfant or Washington, or none recorded an answer. The name suddenly appeared in a letter of Jefferson's in 1791. One theory has it that the designation of the city's primary axis was an appeasement to the state where Congress was then convening. Philadelphia had designs as the new capital city, as did New York, after whose state another great avenue, running northeast from the White House, was also named. Perhaps Pennsylvania, then a buffer between merchant North and planter South, was a compromise choice. Pamela Scott of the Smithsonian Institution's Museum of American History believes that "Pennsylvania" was more likely a product of logical, geographic progression. "The three main streets traversing the city, Massachusetts, Pennsylvania, and Virginia, follow in [descending geographic] sequence," she said. She saw the strong hand of George Washington at work in that progression.

Connecticut Congressman John Cotton Smith came to town with the new government in 1800, and he found the new capital's one and only street "a deep morass covered with elder bushes" and a sidewalk spread from chips off the Capitol "extended but a little way." City commissioners were fussing again, this time about those "who have brick yards in Pennsylvania Avenue which are in the way of the pavers and ditchers." Dismissed by Washington, Pierre L'Enfant was long gone, not from town, where he wandered, cursing his fate and inadequate compensation, but from any planning authority. When Jefferson took office, the new president, himself a habitué of the Champs-Elysées, took a keen interest in the broad, axial avenue. He ordered it planted with four rows of poplars, suggesting a Paris boulevard.

A well-known sketch of the slender, quick-growing Lombardy poplars paints a pastoral, manicured — and utterly fantasied — picture, for in truth the early Avenue was but a cut above a quagmire. A simple walk by members of Congress to Capitol Hill from their rooming houses near Sixth Street was described by Wilhelmus Bogart Bryan as "a matter of personal and unpleasant experiences." The "forlorn as well as unwholesome surrounding of Pennsylvania Avenue in this section were early attributed mainly to the location of the canal" flowing torpidly just to the south. So deep was the mud on the Avenue, so yawning its corduroy furrows — cavernous enough to hide robbers, it was said — that Senator John Eaton of Tennessee declared the Avenue "impassable." Pigs "squealed in mud-rooting glee," wrote the *Star*.

Top: Brown's Indian Queen Hotel was named for a swinging sign that bore a likeness of Pocahontas. It was also called Brown's Marble Hotel for its facade. Guests included John Jacob Astor, Sam Houston, and the Hungarian patriot Louis Kossuth, who brought a retinue of armed guards for a stay in 1851. (The Old Print Shop Inc., Kenneth M. Newman)

Bottom: L'Enfant envisioned a city of "magnificent spaces," with vast open lands between the great nodes of his plan. What he could not have foreseen is that some of those spaces would approximate a barnyard. In this 1839 view, a farmer leads his bare bones of a horse to market on the Avenue. (Library of Congress)

Opposite top: This 1803 view from Market Square shows the old U.S. Patent Office, designed as a hotel by White House architect James Hoban. The new city's first theatrical performance was later held there. Reported one dismayed observer: "The floor was but temporarily laid with rough boards. The seats, also, were all rough boards." (Library of Congress)

Opposite bottom: The Capitol surely looked grand in its circa 1800 isolation. Not so for the setting. In 1806, one observer noted that "half-starved cattle browsing among the bushes present a melancholy spectacle." The Avenue was little more than a muddy path cut through the woods and bushes. (Library of Congress)

Above: An 1839 view from the White House. The Avenue looks as placid and well-mannered as a manorial estate. Actually, these were gritty times of boardinghouses and open sewers. (Engraving by W. H. Bartlett & H. Wallis, Kiplinger Collection)

Left: Horace P. Russ's 1853 proposal to convert the Avenue into a pedestrian mall, replete with checkerboard paving, was never carried out. (Lithograph by Endicott & Co., New York; collection of Columbia Historical Society)

Opposite: Bird's-eye view of the Avenue in 1859 shows the pestiferous City Canal, later paved over to create Constitution Avenue. The Washington Monument is prematurely depicted as finished. The job wasn't done until the 1880s. (Kiplinger Collection)

Lured by promotional excess to come see a model city, a Brasilia of its time, visitors found instead a slatternly, miasmal village. "Some half-starved cattle browsing among the bushes present a melancholy spectacle," observed Charles W. Jansen in 1806. "The nights are so noisy that one can scarcely sleep," griped the Chevalier de Bacourt in 1840. "There is a continual uproar, the reason for which is that the inhabitants all own cows and pigs, but no stables." Women milk their cows right on the sidewalk, he tutted, "and sprinkle the passers-by. The nocturnal wanderings of these beasts create an infernal racket, in which they are joined by dogs and cats."

So turbulent was springtime flooding that President Jefferson himself joined a crowd trying to save three men swept up in the current and clinging to sycamore branches. "Mr. Jefferson felt such anxiety for these unfortunate men," reported Christian Hines, "that he offered fifteen dollars for each person saved, and the use of his horse to anyone who would make the venture to rescue them, but no one attempted it, and they had to remain in their unenviable positions all night." If it wasn't spill-water and mud, it was dust. Urchins worked for tips, sweeping the crossings clean. On a visit in 1793 to lay the cornerstone of the Capitol, President Washington marched ankle-deep in powdery soil at the head of a procession of Masons. Come the Civil War, the footfalls of troops and their steeds kicked up a perpetual haze. *New York Herald* correspondent George B. Wallis, who fancied himself a poet, wrote, in "The Dust Clouds of Old Washington,"

> The slop on the Avenue dries in an hour —
> Invisibly drying, but drying so soon,
> The mud before breakfast is dust before noon.

The White House and Capitol seemed like remote, unrelated mirages. A French traveler, La-Rochefoucault-Liancourt, applauded the view in 1797 but said L'Enfant's plan looked to him like "nothing but a dream." So distant were the incipient edifices of state, he added, that "if the gap is not filled, communications will be impracticable in winter, for one can scarcely suppose that the United States would undergo the expense of pavement, footpaths, and lamps for so long a stretch of uninhabited ground."

Left: Washington went wild in 1871 with the unveiling of a newly paved Avenue — a $2 million project to smooth it over with wood blocks, which were swept as clean as a parlor floor for a two-day celebration. But the jubilation didn't last. Horses and carts tore the boulevard to splinters in no time. (Washingtoniana Division, D.C. Public Library)

Above: The Avenue's low profile of 1872 afforded a great look at the Washington Monument, then rising as slowly as a great redwood. (Columbia Historical Society)

Right: A bond issue for the 1870s Avenue repaving. (Library of Congress)

When the elements did not deter the pursuit of happiness, rogues did. Richard Lee wrote: "The denizens of Washington's underworld, thieves, illegal liquor vendors, touts, prostitutes and the like, would envelop [Union soldiers] like flies. Most of the innocents were soon fleeced of their $13-a-month pay and returned to camp sadder and wiser men."

By the end of its first century, Washington still did not have a main street worth bothering to see. Sneered *Harper's Weekly* in 1890, "There is a shabby decay visible to the most unobservant eye. The structures make no sky-line at all; the avenue is so wide and they are so low that they form simply raised edges, as it were, to the outlines of the street." When Washington is called the nation's most beautiful city, added the magazine, "Pennsylvania Avenue is not included in the flattering unction."

Above: Progress had visited the Avenue by 1907. Its name was asphalt. A repair crew at work near Tenth Street. (James M. Goode Collection, Library of Congress)

Right: Winter at the National Capitol, drawn by Charles Graham for *Harper's Weekly,* March 7, 1895. (Kiplinger Collection)

Above: An 1839 vista showing one of the first train routes alongside Tiber Creek. Said diarist Margaret Bayard Smith in 1800, "The Tiber! The Capitol! were words which imparted charm to every surrounding object." Few shared her enthusiasm. (Library of Congress)

Right: Tiber Creek looks like a rustic brook refreshing the Irish slum of Swampoodle, but by 1850 the waterway and its canal had degenerated into "an indescribable cesspool" full of "smells and malarial mosquitos." By 1908 both the creek and Swampoodle were a memory, filled in and paved over for Union Station and its train yards. (Washingtoniana Division, D.C. Public Library)

Charnel Along the Tiber and a Road Made of Iron

To tidewater people, a "creek" did not amount to much. Skimpy tentacles meandered from distant hillsides, but the brunt of it was a stubby thumb that opened into a river or bay. Clogged by runoffs of velvety alluvial soil and prone to flooding, it was nearly useless for commerce. But its very indolence made a creek ripe for taming, and to that end L'Enfant laid his plans for Tiber Creek.

The Tiber, or "Tyber," began as three small runs, the largest forming on the grounds of the Soldiers' Home above Boundary Avenue in the hills north of town. Its main tine babbled along cowpaths, blackberry patches, and, eventually, the B&O Railroad track, past Reedbirds' Hill at M Street, and then south through a humble gristmill before bumping into Capitol Hill, where it bent southwest and fell across Pennsylvania Avenue at Second Street. Suddenly tidal, it flattened, fishhooked north for a few hundred yards, then jerked acutely to the west, paralleling the Avenue, and lolled toward the Potomac. It gradually widened into its thumb, which met the river. There, where the Tiber deposited the town's richest soil, that stubborn early planter, David Burnes, had built his cabin in the mid-1700s, and overlooking the inlet, architect Benjamin Latrobe would raise the mighty Van Ness mansion in 1810. From both houses, you could see Braddock's Rock slightly up the Potomac. Steamboats later docked at the Tiber mouth before churning for Alexandria.

At its headwaters Francis Pope, an early member of the Maryland General Assembly, had carved his "Rome" plantation in the 1600s. The run was Goose Creek then, but who could resist completing the classical allegory by renaming it? A creek through Pope's Rome had to be . . . the Tiber!

L'Enfant paced the path along the stream below the Avenue and saw the makings of a grand canal. According to architectural historian Ernest Connally, "At one time it was conceived that the President would go in a state barge from the White House up this canal to Congress." So it was as a canal that L'Enfant drew the tidal Tiber, considerably straightened, from Third Street west to the river, and a canal it would become, though hardly grand. Water was a favorite ornament of French gardens and of his vision for Washington, and L'Enfant pictured a cooling cascade trilling down the Capitol's west hillside. The Tiber would feed it from the north, and the waterscape would in turn freshen the canal.

The Tiber's banks were thick with sycamore roots and turtle nests. An early resident, Hines, remembered shooting wild ducks along its inlet. "People used to throw stones at them," he wrote. Upstream, at a vacant lot near Reedbirds' Hill, the Post Office destroyed its "dead letters," drawing a sizable crowd, eager to paw for coins and trinkets. Where it crossed the Avenue, the Tiber bed had dug a formidable ditch.

Spring freshets turned the slothful Tiber angry. Then, reported the *Washington Times*, "it was not unusual for persons to fall over or drive their teams over the bank and into the water at this point" on the Avenue. Hackman Paddy Welch and his team were drowned there. At the same place, the *Times* continued, "the Tiber was sometimes utilized by the fire laddies of that day to deposit each other's apparatus when captured during their little dissentions." It must have been quite a view, gazing across the Tiber and up the Avenue toward the President's House. Upon her arrival in Washington in 1800, diarist Margaret Bayard Smith exuded, "The Tiber! The Capitol! were words which imparted charm to every surrounding object."

Except at flood tide, the sliver of high ground between Pennsylvania Avenue and the Tiber was spongy-dry, though Hines noted that the creek flattened into a "large sheet of water," stretching as far north as (and all too often across) the Avenue, at Seventh. "The Island" of dry ground would one day support the city's most notorious precincts: a freedmen's settlement, gaming halls, the taverns of Murder Bay, and Hooker's Division houses of the evening. Don't fall for the tale that the dollies therein took their name from General Joe Hooker, however. Washington architect and historian Donald A. Hawkins reported that prostitutes had been "hookers" long before the commander "got stuck overseeing men who were interested in them."

In 1903 Daniel Burnham supervised the building of a colossal union train station over the Tiber's former creek bed in the decrepit Irish Swampoodle neighborhood north of the Avenue. By that time, the city's favorite garbage dump had petered to a trickle.

Construction for L'Enfant's grand canal began in 1807. South and west of Pennsylvania Avenue, the canal became Washington's sewer of choice — larger, someone snorted, than the greatest sewer in Paris. When he was promoting it, Thomas Law had gushed, "Should this canal be finished, Washington need not envy London its Thames." At the canal's completion in 1815, the Marine Band followed a vessel for two hours from Twelfth Street to the Eastern Branch. In 1837 the City Canal would connect at Tiber Inlet with the Chesapeake & Ohio Canal, heading to Georgetown and on to "the West." But the undercapitalized canal company shored most of the Tiber canal's length with wood, which rotted repeatedly; company dredgers were hard-pressed to keep ahead of siltation, and floods kept whisking goods off the wharves. The city was fast growing out of its beguilement with water transit.

Residents reckoned the Tiber and its canal were the source of "agues and bilious fevers causing a high death rate," wrote Frederick Gutheim in *Worthy of the Nation*. Even presidents fled its "smells and malarial mosquitos" to highland country estates, he added. "An indescribable cesspool," someone else called it. Malaria and "collery" tormented the populace, chiefly, wrote Alfred Mason Badger in 1832, "Irish men that are at work . . . Macadamizing the avenue." According to Margaret Leech in *Reveille in Washington*, bodies of Union soldiers killed at the Battle of Ball's Bluff, near Leesburg, Virginia, washed down the Potomac and as far into the Tiber Inlet as the Sixth Street wharf. Butchers at the Center Market routinely dumped poultry innards, rotted fish, and animal carcasses straight into the canal. Little wonder it became known as the B Street Main.

Left: Troops drilling in the rain near the Tiber in 1861. The creek's regular flooding drove merchants up the hill to F Street, which developed as an upscale shopping district. (Library of Congress)

Right: Joseph Hooker (here photographed by Mathew Brady) could not take credit for renaming the oldest profession, but his men certainly partook of the service economy peculiar to the locale of their Avenue encampment. (National Portrait Gallery)

Below: The foul City Canal (shown turning away from the almost-finished Capitol dome) sludges toward the Potomac. (Library of Congress)

This likeness of Governor Alexander "Boss" Shepherd has withstood time with more dignity than his Avenue statue, which was shunted off to "storage" at a city sewage plant. In the 1870s the planner of $6.25 million worth of public improvements — including the planting of fifty thousand trees and laying of twenty-three miles of new sewers — was exposed for corruption and disgraced by Congress. In 1887 he returned to ride in a hero's parade down the Avenue. Gentlemen wore high silk hats, and John Philip Sousa led the Marine Band. From among the crowd of one hundred thousand rose the cry, "Three cheers for the maker of Washington!" (PADC)

B Street itself began as a path along the canal, but it became a rutted dirt street following the huge fire of 1870 at the market. As part of a city construction blitz a year later, Boss Shepherd set work gangs to filling and covering the "pestiferous" canal and running a pipe to make it a true sewer. A procession of dingy buildings, including the Pennsylvania Railroad's terminal and train sheds, would rise on B Street. In the midst of Federal Triangle construction, to mark George Washington's two hundredth birthday in 1932, B Street would be renamed Constitution Avenue.

In his picturesque white beard, Wisconsin Representative Henry Allen Cooper orated that the "soon-to-be beautiful avenue" linking the Capitol grounds and Arlington Cemetery across the new Arlington Memorial Bridge, would "in sentiment unite" North and South. Crews laying the Federal Triangle's foundations turned up old Tiber wharves, early U.S. coins, and the discards of several generations. In 1935, V. Y. Dove, who held a contract for demolishing a seventy-two-foot strip of the old Tiber under Pennsylvania Avenue, called the subterranean brook "the greatest nuisance in Washington." A newspaper of the time found janitors casting for carp through gratings in the Capitol basement — an unlikely tale, since the streambed trickled two blocks away. The Tiber Inlet at the Potomac was soon no more, either. Over several decades, government engineers filled it to create West Potomac Park and the Lincoln Memorial reflecting pool.

The Tiber had already become mostly a memory. "It must be an old resident of this city who can recall the Tiber in its palmy days," wrote the *Washington Times* in 1901, "when citizens bathed in its refreshing waters in summer or skated on its congealed surface in winter." All that would remind Washington of the Tiber eighty-seven years later were the stone lockkeeper's house, still standing at Seventeenth and Constitution; a cluster of condominiums called Tiber Island (there was no island); a construction company; and a pub that had adopted the name. A plaque marking the spot of Braddock's Rock could still be found, with some effort. It lay shaved and submerged, fifteen feet down a manhole, on an approach ramp to the Theodore Roosevelt Bridge.

Above: The only vestige of City Canal is this lockkeeper's house, now cleaned up and a fixture among the monuments at Seventeenth and Constitution. (Library of Congress)

Left: Construction along the Avenue in 1948 uncovered these water-main logs from the Tiber Creek era. Note the Apex Liquors building (now Sears House) and the city bus, a symbol of trackless days to come. (Columbia Historical Society)

Right: The Baltimore & Ohio's first Avenue depot was in this converted tailor's shop near Second Street. The B&O attached a belfry to the structure to alert its Washington customers of departures. In this era before the advent of standard time, Baltimore and Washington clocks were set ten or fifteen minutes apart. (Washingtoniana Division, D.C. Public Library)

Below: A steam train of the Alexandria & Washington railroad pulls up to the Capitol, circa 1866. The noise, heat, and cinders of the trains disgusted some legislators, but it took covert action by Boss Shepherd to remove the rails that crossed the Avenue. He simply ordered the offending track torn up, and it was done overnight. (Sketch by F. Dielman from *Harper's Weekly,* April 28, 1866, Kiplinger Collection)

Opposite: This 1864 B&O placard promised SPEED, SECURITY and COMFORT, important considerations for the Civil War–era travelers worried about Confederate acts of sabotage. (Columbia Historical Society)

An intrusion into the capital's early tranquillity that proved almost as pernicious as Tiber Creek and its canal was the coming of the railroad in 1835, along the Tiber and right up to Pennsylvania Avenue. At first the iron horse touched off such civic rapture that George Washington's adopted son, Washington Parke Custis, wrote an operetta about it. One of its songs began,

> Of each wonderful plan
> E'er invented by man,
> That which nearest perfection approaches
> Is a road made of iron,
> Which horses ne'er tire on
> And traveled by steam, in steam coaches.

A stagecoach ride from Willard's or Brown's Indian Queen hotels to Bladensburg, in the briars of Maryland, and on to Baltimore, had taken ten bumpy hours and sustained the cash drawers of several grogshops and wayside houses. The Baltimore & Ohio's new twelve-horsepower steam engines covered the same course in two-and-a-half hours. No wonder nearly a thousand citizens and "two bands of Music" gathered to hail the first four engines — shrewdly christened the Washington, Adams, Jefferson, and Madison—as they pulled into the makeshift depot at Henry Morfit's converted boardinghouse hard by the Tiber on the Avenue, two blocks from the Capitol. For a time, the trains were such a curiosity that citizens walked from distant points just to see the steam cars. Until hackers and gawkers got used to the huffing machines, trains stopped at the city line and were pulled by horses to the new depot. For a time thereafter, a flagman on horseback rode ahead of the behemoths to warn citizens of their coming.

Jubilation did not last long in the halls of Congress. Not only did members find the serenity of their rooming houses disturbed by the racket of the depot, their official deliberations were ruffled as well, each time the stationmaster proclaimed a departure by clanging a huge bell. A resolution soon declared the station "a nuisance, where the idle gathered." The railroad obligingly moved off the Avenue in 1851, but only because its six daily departures and bustling freight business warranted larger quarters. If anything, the locomotives' intrusion into the deliberative process worsened, as the B&O relocated even closer to the Capitol, at New Jersey Avenue and C Street. The idle then gathered at the former depot for sure, when it reopened as a saloon.

But trains were not gone from Pennsylvania Avenue for long. With an eye toward connecting

with southern lines across the Long Bridge, and with a wink from Congress, the railroad stretched a spur smack across the Avenue, practically at the Capitol's west door. There was even talk, soon squelched, of running a track midway up the Avenue to the City Canal turning basin. There trains would tap both freight bounty off the river and burgeoning banking business at the city's emerging commercial hub. Troops by the thousands billeted and drilled in Washington during the Civil War, marching down the Avenue to the B&O station; so, in lesser numbers and at the point of bayonets, did a "Rogues' March" of handcuffed pickpockets, tagged with signs announcing their offense. They were given tickets, one-way, as far as Philadelphia.

One railroad's batch of belching engines was indignity enough. In 1873, having talked Congress into granting it fourteen acres of public grounds on the Mall, the B&O's fierce rival, the Pennsylvania, engineered a neat end run into town as well. A new Pennsy subsidiary, the Baltimore & Potomac, grafted a twenty-mile stem onto an obscure line through southern Maryland and built its own somber terminal next to Center Market at Sixth Street, half a block south of Pennsylvania Avenue. Eight years later, President James A. Garfield would be shot and mortally wounded there. Once he had died, following an agonizing dissipation, the Pennsy marked with a star the spot where Charles J. Guiteau had struck.

By then, the motley combination of the B&O's rails across the Avenue; the B&P's grimy train sheds, track tines, and coal yards; and a jungle of gardens and paths had turned L'Enfant's Mall into an urban rat's nest. Finally swept into the fervor of City Beautiful reform—and after protracted battles

between aesthetes and supporters of railroad suzerainty—congressional leaders in 1903 ordered both rail companies to retrench—the Pennsy south, out of the Mall, and B&O north, away from their delicate sensibilities. But Daniel Burnham, fortuitously positioned as both the Pennsy's architect and ramrod of the greens-keeping Senate Park Commission, got Pennsy President Alexander Cassatt to go Congress one step grander. The Pennsylvania had just wrenched control of the B&O, so Burnham proposed that they share a "union station," still in sight but out of earshot of the Capitol, along Massachusetts Avenue in decrepit Swampoodle. Deal, replied Cassatt, if the government would finance a tunnel under Capitol Hill, so long-haul trains could connect with the South. The Union Station, modeled after the Baths of Diocletian in Rome, that would rise atop the odorous remains of Tiber Creek would be so immense that, it was averred, the nation's entire standing army of fifty thousand men could form ranks in its barrel-vaulted concourse. The last train left the old B&O yards on October 27, 1907, and the Pennsylvania terminal slammed its doors shut a month later.

Rails of a different sort had stretched the length of the Avenue for forty-five years. The Washington and Georgetown Railroad Company ran horse cars on rails — far less jarring than the washboard road over which omnibuses had jangled. "Herds of cattle, and sometimes long columns of marching men, surrounded the new streetcars on all sides," wrote Lee in *Mr. Lincoln's City*. In 1892, the company replaced the horses and their pungent pollution problem (a certain source of lockjaw, it was said) with an innovative underground cable system that, minus the hills, was a ringer for San Francisco's. The whirling cables emanated from the Washington and Georgetown's giant powerhouse at Fourteenth Street and the Avenue. Giant wheels tugged the cables, one stretching east to the Navy Yard, the other west to Georgetown. Where horses had lugged coaches at three miles per hour, grip cars clinging to the cable and pulling a passenger trailer whizzed along at three times that speed.

But at 11:15 the night of September 29, 1897, the company's powerhouse burst into flames, the fire stoked by oily rags, wooden furniture, and company files. As it burned, Washington and Georgetown officials hustled up the C&O canal, buying horses; the next morning, passengers were greeted by their usual cable cars, but pulled by horses connected to hastily assembled whiffletrees. The cables never again turned, for within a year, the company installed an electrical system, carrying six hundred volts of direct current in the old cable conduit, eighteen inches underground. What the trainmen called a "plow" beneath the streetcars grabbed power from a third rail through a slit in the pavement.

Through more than six decades of electric-streetcar service, Pennsylvania Avenue never saw a trolley wire. Cars would rattle along the Avenue with their power poles laid flat. At transition points elsewhere throughout the city, two men would connect the cars to overhead power. In a flash, one worker perched in a pit beneath the street would disengage the plow, while another hoisted the power pole. Raised concrete stands lined most streetcar stops, but on the Avenue the stands were wooden. "Deep moans of anguish usually emanate from the District Building at the thought of moving the heavy, wooden streetcar loading platforms to make way for a parade," wrote the *Star* in 1947. But there was always the chance to pocket coins that had dropped between platform slats.

Opposite: "The assassin firing the second shot at President Garfield" in the Baltimore & Potomac terminal (above) next to Center Market, on July 2, 1881. Garfield was heading out of town for a seaside break at Elberon, New Jersey. The stricken president later went to Elberon to recover, but he died about ten weeks after the shooting. The railroad marked with a star the spot where Charles J. Guiteau had struck. (Drawn by W. A. Rogers, collection of Smithsonian Institution)

Above: Streetcar lines and a cluster of hotels grew up around the depot of the Pennsylvania Railroad subsidiary, the Baltimore & Potomac, near Center Market at Sixth and B streets, N.W. The Pennsy's brooding station and its train sheds and tracks compounded the jumble on the Mall, which was already cluttered with trees, residences, small shops and stables and was anything but the open grounds with their vast vistas that we know today. The longer of the two streetcar coaches grabbed power via a "plow" that slipped through a slot in the street and ran along a third, electrified rail underground. (LeRoy O. King Collection)

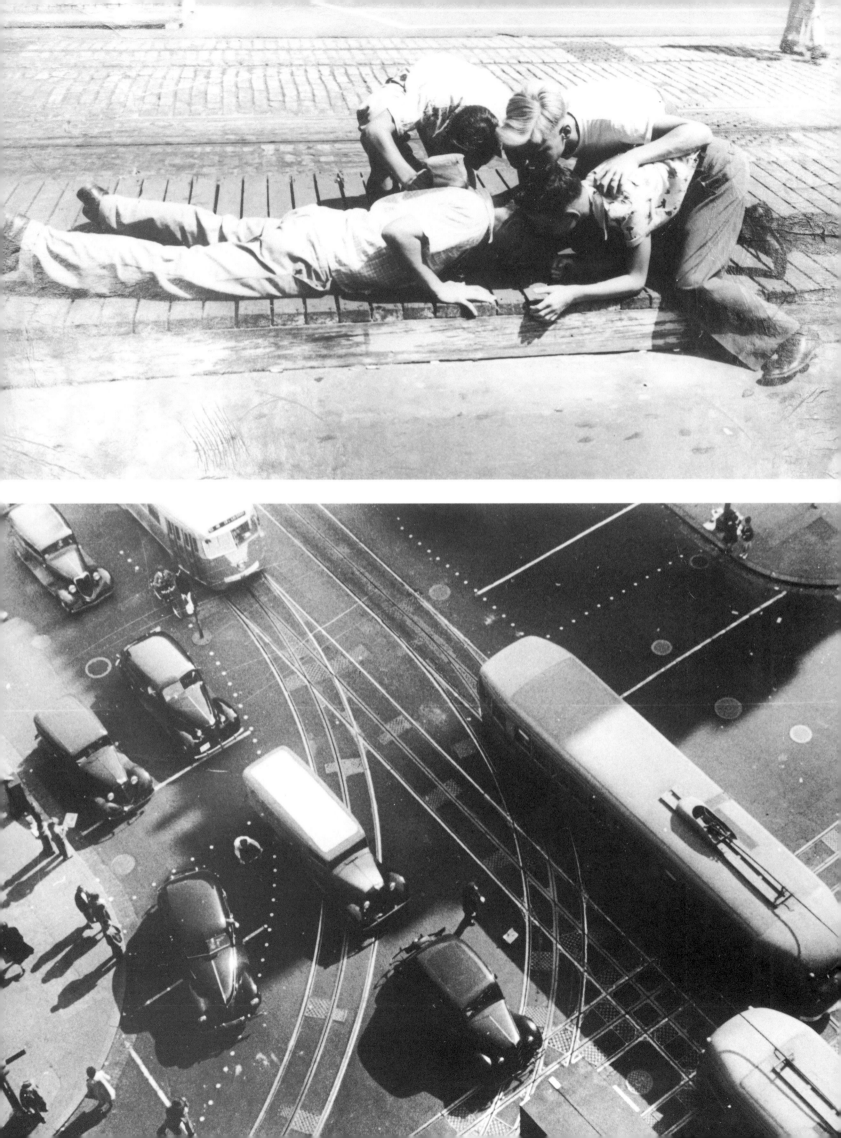

By 1950, the Pennsylvania Avenue streetcar route (fare, twenty cents) was reported to be the second-most-profitable in America, behind the Forty-second Street line in New York. With the building of the Federal Triangle, streetcars in endless procession accepted and disgorged government workers. But modernist sentiment in the press and in Congress began to inveigh against the clangoring cars. "I wonder if it may not be expedient to replace the present unsightly street car platforms and tracks with an up-to-date bus service," in order to make Pennsylvania "the most beautiful avenue in the world," asked Illinois Representative Fred Britten in letters to just about every public commission in town. In 1931, General Mason M. Patrick, head of the Public Utilities Commission, proposed tunneling a subway beneath the Avenue to help loosen traffic, already snarled and sure to worsen as the Triangle complex reached completion. It would not be until the late 1970s, though, that a subway would skitter under the Avenue, two lines stopping at the Triangle and another across from the National Archives.

In vain, Capital Transit Company owner O. Roy Chalk extolled the economies of streetcars over buses. He even ran an experimental air-conditioned rail coach past the Capitol. Fittingly, the last streetcar to run in Washington, on January 28, 1962, clanked from Fourteenth Street to the Navy Yard along Pennsylvania Avenue.

Opposite top: These 1940s boys were exploring the depths of the Avenue's wooden streetcar platforms, possibly looking for change that could whisk them off to a Senators baseball game. (Washingtoniana Division, D.C. Public Library)

Opposite bottom: This arresting 1939 view of Fourteenth Street and the Avenue illustrates the streetcars with their power poles tucked in. There were no overhead power lines on the Avenue — a price transit workers paid for with the dangerous task of connecting a "plow" to a third rail buried in the pavement. (Library of Congress)

Above left: O. Roy Chalk, the transit baron who introduced air-cooled streetcars in a last-ditch effort to save the rolling stock. (Washington Star Collection, D.C. Public Library)

Above right: Congress thought the streetcars and their platforms unsightly. The legislators preferred buses. Bedecked with banners as though they were part of a great procession, the last streetcars rolled on the Avenue on January 28, 1962. (LeRoy King, Jr. Collection)

Above: A transit strike in 1955 gave the Avenue a taste of traffic jams to come. (D.C. Public Library)

Right: In the 1970s Metro brought trains to the Avenue again, this time well underground. (Carol M. Highsmith)

Shucking at Harvey's and Jiving at Kann's

Well before John Adams moved to town in 1800, peddlers had thrown up stalls across from the unfinished President's House. Soon shopping activities gravitated to what the locals called the Marsh Market — more formally, Centre (later Center) Market, between Seventh and Ninth Streets on the Avenue — blocking L'Enfant's cherished vista from the (never-built) pantheon to the river. Seventh Street was the key link between the Washington waterfront and the Bladensburg Road turnpike to Baltimore. Tuesdays, Thursdays, and Saturdays became "market days" — and swapping and gossiping days — at Market Square. There, David Ballie Warden wrote in 1816, "Two of the luxuries of life, pine-apples and ice, are found . . . at a cheap rate." Across the river, gunshots resounded through the woods of Virginia, as hunters bagged turkeys, quail, and ducks to take to market, and Potomac shad and herring, "noted for their lusciousness," were marketed off boats at the turning basin of the City Canal. In 1890, *Illustrated Washington* called Center Market "in many particulars, the market, par excellence, of the country," where "throngs of buyers of all classes of society, fashionable women of the West End, accompanied by negro servants, mingled with people of less opulent sections."

Even in 1988, Libby Rowe, who had chaired the National Capital Planning Commission in the 1960s, remembered Center Market as a place where "people fried their rabbits and chickens and ate outside." Harrison Lee said the people down the Avenue at Chinatown would buy chickens at the market, carry the squawking fowl home, and pen them on porches for slaughter and Chinese-style cooking throughout the week.

Opposite: Recalled a longtime Washingtonian, when they razed Center Market in 1931 to build the National Archives, the streets were flooded with rats. Mathew Brady made this photo from the window of his studio. (Library of Congress)

Below: The bakery department of Center Market in 1915. (James M. Goode Collection, Library of Congress)

Left: In 1865, Old Hay Market teemed with butchers and greengrocers on a site where Justice Department bureaucrats now roam. The Canterbury Hotel was destroyed in 1871. (Columbia Historical Society)

Below: Metzerott Hall (with piano sign) in 1879. The music store struck a sour note in 1894, when its cast-iron facade fell, killing a clerk. (Library of Congress)

Right: Tuesdays, Thursdays, and Saturdays were "market days" — and thus swapping and gossip days — at old Market Square. A circa 1900 view. (Columbia Historical Society)

Both the market and the facing north-side block, called Market Space, teemed with more than butchers and greengrocers. Dry-goods dealers, glassworks, tanners, and even two woolen mills sprang up there. Some of the city's first black-owned hotels, shops, and restaurants, including Beverly Snow's Epicurean Eating House, took root near Market Square. Wagon trains clogged the Avenue, fist fights abounded, and, wrote Richard Lee, "a growing number of embalming establishments appeared near the Market. Stacks of wooden coffins, upended on the sidewalk, announced their presence." The parlors did a brisk wartime business. Lee quoted the *Daily Chronicle*, "It insults the meanest animals to have their dead and food in juxtaposition!"

Pennsylvania Avenue also saw humans — gangs of shackled slaves — as commodities led to auction. Guests at Avenue hotels were invited to keep their human chattel chained in the basement while they moved about the city.

By midcentury, Pennsylvania Avenue had its first water main (1832), gas lamps (1853), house numbers (1854), horse-drawn streetcars (1862), and smallpox epidemic (1862). According to the institutional history of the Woodward & Lothrop department store, which opened as Boston Dry Goods on the Avenue in 1880, heavier industries, except those "that drew their permanence from government connections or contracts," did not last. Washington's was a "service economy" even then. One of the first blocks offered by the new federal government for private purchase, between Third and Fourth streets, was called Bank Square. When commercial activity grew around Center Market, banks, including Lewis Johnson & Company, Franklin National (overlooking Ben's statue), and Central National, clustered across the Avenue.

Above: Banks proliferated along the commercial Avenue in the nineteenth century. In 1894 the ornate NS&T Bank towered over the confluence of Fifteenth Street and Pennsylvania and New York avenues. Within a few years the massive neo-Roman facade of Riggs would rise on the opposite corner. (Raymond Sayers)

Right: An 1890 view of the Romanesque National Bank of Washington and the twin-towered Apex Liquors building (now Sears House). The towers were added by Alfred B. Mullett, architect for the Old Executive Office Building. Mathew Brady's photographic studio was next door. (James M. Goode Collection, Library of Congress)

Opposite: Detail of the National Bank of Washington building. (Carol M. Highsmith)

Above: An 1890s view of Tenth Street reveals that our ancestors were as enamored of clutter as today's billboard advocates. (Culver Pictures)

Right: The flood of 1889 — result of the same spring rains that swamped Johnstown, Pennsylvania — brought back memories of the Tiber's excesses. (Columbia Historical Society)

"Pennsylvania Avenue is not the oldest street in the world — it merely looks so," wrote the *Post* in 1911. "It is true that back in 1880 a merchant painted the front of his store. Feeling ran high against him, but he averted trouble by leaving town." The *Post* noted, with relief, that "the price of whisky has not changed on the avenue since Jackson was President." The article recounted the history of Shoomaker's saloon, which "changes nothing except your money." The joint specialized in "perpendicular drinks," the paper reported. "One may sit down at Shoomaker's, but one would rather not. Those who are on their feet when the building falls down will have a much better chance of getting out." The *Star* observed that "unfortunately, the city paved the avenue some time ago and thus robbed it of its one time distinction of being the worst street in the world." Flooding had driven many prosperous merchants to higher ground on F Street by 1900, but passersby still idled at the Evening Star and Washington Post buildings to catch up on current events or watch the inning-by-inning posting of baseball scores.

The "Historical and Commercial Sketches" of the Avenue in 1884 listed Barber & Ross door and sash dealers, who specialized in mantels; the Maison Doree "elegant and faultless" restaurant, where "their supply of cigars is most elegant, and the most fastidious smoker will find that the world has been put under contribution to gratify his taste"; Allison Nailor Livery Stables, run by "a graduate of the Royal Veterinary College in Prussia"; and Thos. O. Hills, D.D.S., where "anaesthetics are used with the best effect." Street-sweepers in white uniforms and helmets added a picturesque touch to the Avenue. An apothecary at Twelfth and the Avenue dispensed fizzy "colored water" from vats that caught both the sun through the window and an admiring crowd. In a frame building up the Avenue, C. Gauthier ran a restaurant and confectionary called "Ala Ville de Paris." Across the street, Lewis Carusi opened a "dancing saloon," which became one of the city's popular theaters. For the twelve years from 1841 to 1853, the city post office was located in Carusi's basement.

By mid-nineteenth century, "Government offices closed at three," wrote the President's Council on Pennsylvania Avenue in the historical portion of its 1964 report.

Federal employees and the rest of the city's inhabitants descended onto the Avenue to promenade, ride, see and be seen, imbibe, shop, and meet friends to take home to tea. Color abounded as costumed foreign diplomats, delegations of [American] Indians, and a variety of visitors from outside parts mingled with uniformed officers who, perhaps waiting while their ladies shopped for laces, ribbons, and gloves, could spend their time gazing at the constellations through sidewalk telescopes or testing their lung capacities at the lung-testing machine.

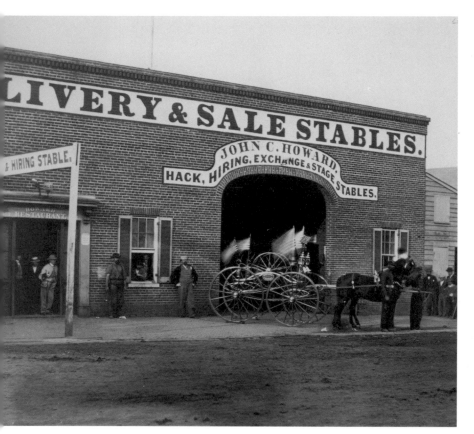

Above left: The Avenue stable where Booth bought a horse in his escape attempt after shooting Lincoln. The actor called for his steed from his window at the National Hotel. Inaugural bunting was still draped over many Avenue buildings. (Library of Congress)

Above right: John Wilkes Booth in 1865. (Library of Congress)

Right: A block eventually razed for the FBI Building, which displaced one hundred small merchants. Pictured is the Central Building, whose tenants included a dentist, a drug store, money-lenders, insurance agents, jewelers, and tobacconists. (Columbia Historical Society)

Above: Horse-drawn street-cleaning trucks near the Capitol in 1905. (PADC)

Left: Police used some of the Avenue's earliest telephones while suffragists marched in the background. (Washingtoniana Division, D.C. Public Library)

There were no department stores in those days. According to Charles Noble, people "never dreamed of buying books or furniture or ready-made clothing at the same place with dress goods or jewelry." Rival members of the Willard family ran three separate hotels, Willard's, the Occidental, and the Ebbitt House. The crush of customers at Harvey's restaurant began in 1862, during the Civil War, when troops discovered a delicacy: steamed clams. Wrote Thomas R. Henry, "A large iron pot was set up in the center of the shop, where clams were boiled and dished out as rapidly as the attendants could handle them." Because of the rush to serve the tasty bivalves, Harvey's took to steaming the clams, with delectable results. A crowded raw-oyster bar was set up in one corner, and "hundreds of men in blue uniforms stretched down the Avenue, waiting for their turn to get in. The shucking beds extended along Eleventh, B, and C Streets, forming three sides of a hollow square." Abe Lincoln once ordered his carriage stopped to taste the "new and delicious dish" and was reported "well satisfied." Signs saying Honest Abe Shucked

Here, or words to that effect, spurred business. Harvey's became a Federal Triangle project casualty in the 1930s but moved elsewhere in the city.

So, too, did many professional offices and prime businesses, to swankier quarters along K Street near Dupont Circle, or in Georgetown, following World War II. But smaller shops hung on. D. J. Kaufman's clothier, technically on D Street, but facing the Avenue, proposed erecting a turquoise facade with aluminum trim, but the Fine Arts Commission, which the *Star* said "seems to be against anything unusual in Washington," rejected the outrage; the panels became walnut and beige instead. Acme Liquor Store prospered, celebrating fifty years in 1957. Kann's, once a brimming, midpriced department store that lured streetcar shoppers from around the area, saw an immediate downturn in business and an abrupt change to an inner-city clientele following the riots of 1968. By then, Pierre L'Enfant's planned promenade route had changed—it seemed irretrievably at the time—into an urban contradiction: a forbidding federal wall to the south and classic decay to the north.

Opposite left: An 1849 ad for the United States Hotel, which stood between Third and Four-and-a-half streets, "one square above the rail road depot." The area from Third to Seventh streets became known as Hash Row for its procession of boardinghouses. In the mid-nineteenth century, their tenants included Chief Justice Roger B. Taney and two of his associate justices on the U.S. Supreme Court. (James M. Goode Collection, Library of Congress)

Opposite right: One fan of Harvey's bivalves was cartoonist Thomas Nast, who drew this affectionate caricature of the porcine proprietor. (James M. Goode Collection, Library of Congress)

Above: A parade floats past Harvey's, which became the rage of wartime Washington, serving up steamed clams by the bucketful and up to five hundred gallons of steamed oysters at a time. Management was even able to boast, "Honest Abe Shucked Here." (Library of Congress)

Pathway of the Presidents

There was a time, several quadrennia ago, when the Greatest Show in Washington was not a rock concert or a congressional investigation. It was an inaugural parade, best viewed from a rented window in the Corcoran Building, or the Southern Railway offices, or GAR Hall. Inaugurals drew "a roaring mob," druggist C. L. Tschiffely told the *Washington Daily News* in 1937. "I've seen people get so drunk on the roofs that they practically have to be taken down with a block and tackle." So long were the parades, shopkeeper Lewis Naiman swore, that spectators would get tired and go home before the show was over, rented perch or not. Even today, old-timers recall crawling out of an Albee Building window onto the marquee of Keith's Theater and watching the tanks, left over from World War I, rumbling behind Calvin Coolidge when he *really* got to be

president in 1925. The caterpillar treads of the thundering machines clunked and crunched over the cobblestones, and if the kids had wanted to, they could have bopped them—or Mr. Coolidge—with an apple.

Inaugurals were far more extemporaneous then: no tickets from Ticketron, no credentialed photo opportunities, just a day to have a snortin' good time on the Avenue, holding Father's hand. How might the Secret Service react today to the cowboy who rode right up to the presidential box and asked if he could toss a lariat around Ike's outstretched hand? Guess who'd be hog-tied. Was that 1977 walk up the Avenue by Jimmy Carter peanut-farmer hokum? Maybe, thought some in the crowd. The ones who'd parked their pickup trucks out in Silver Spring thought it made the tingle even tinglier—so much the better for vendors of peanut banks, peanut tie tacks, and maps of Plains, Georgia.

Opposite: William McKinley's four-mile-long inaugural parade traversed the Avenue on March 4, 1897. The *Evening Star* reported that "[McKinley's] pale face lightened with pleasure." The artist derived this painting from a series of stereopticon slides. (Frank Wright)

Left: Where were you in '53? Ike's top-down inaugural, replete with white Cadillac, sums up 1950s zeitgeist. He took the oath on two bibles, one a gift from his mother and the other one that George Washington used when he was sworn in as the nation's first president. (Dwight D. Eisenhower Library)

Below: Jimmy Carter's "new age" inauguration failed to discourage this Uncle Sam look-alike from engaging in some old-time misanthropy. (Jimmy Carter Library)

Above: This 1829 depiction of Andrew Jackson's inauguration looks more like a coronation. Inaugurals drew roaring mobs for parades so long that they wore out their observers. Not Old Hickory and his band of cavorting pioneers, though. They partied right into the White House, mashing food and drink into the silk damask upholstery, and spreading everywhere the remains of a fourteen-hundred-pound wheel of cheese. (PADC)

Opposite top: Lincoln's rather tentative 1861 inaugural parade consisted mostly of troops. Crowds were thin and subdued. Accompanied by Buchanan, Lincoln rode from his lodgings at Willard's to his inauguration at the Capitol on March 4, 1861. In the parade was a float — draped in red, white, and blue — that carried two young girls wearing laurel-wreath crowns, which symbolized liberty, the states, and the territories. (Kiplinger Collection)

Opposite bottom: George A. Custer, the dashing colonel the Indians called Yellow Hair, created quite a spectacle during the Grand Army's victory march down the Avenue in 1865. His horse was festooned with flowers. A young lady in the crowd threw Custer yet another bouquet, scaring the animal and sending it bucking. (Mathew Brady, National Portrait Gallery)

Thomas Jefferson started something when he, his secretary, and a groom rode up to the Capitol, hitched their horses, and got the oath-taking over in a whipstitch in 1805. It was on the ride back, when friends, a few congressmen, and some "strangers of distinction" rode along with him, that Jefferson began a tradition on the Avenue. Stuffy Madison made it all proper four years later. Old Hickory Jackson and Old Tippecanoe Harrison — the coonskin-cap presidents were always Old Something-or-Other—brought out the hard-cider crowd. Frolicking frontiersmen practiced their Jacksonian Democracy by following Andy right into the White House, mashing food and drink into the silk damask upholstery. Harrison, atop Old Whitey (even his *horse* was Old), doffed his cap so gallantly, and so often, that he caught the grippe that bitter March morning, and a month later it was his funeral cortege that traversed the route. Mrs. Fillmore died the same way, minus the doffing, days after she and her husband had wished new president Pierce Godspeed.

Zach Taylor's big moment fell on a Sunday in 1849, so he let James K. Polk have an extra day on the job, preferring to take the oath first thing

Monday. Lincoln's two parades were as different as North and South. He'd slunk into town under Allan Pinkerton's sharp eye the night before the first one, and when he left Willard's to join Buchanan for the ride to the Capitol, his carriage was surrounded by troops. The buildings were festooned with riflemen, the crowds thin and subdued. Four years and a terrible war later, there were more escorts still, but patriot's gusto was given its head in the crowd. A month later, the body of the murdered president traveled the Avenue again. "Despite the enormous crowd," reported a newspaper of the time, "the silence was profound." All the more reason the march of two-hundred thousand Grand Army veterans over two days drew thankful cheers so loud you could hear them in Georgetown. George A. Custer, the dashing colonel the Indians would call Yellow Hair, was "literally covered with floral offerings," wrote C. C. Collins in *The New Age* magazine. "Inaugural parades will continue, military pageants will be seen and the Avenue will be gay with banners and music, and thronged with marching men," F. J. Young wrote in 1907, "but they will not be the veterans whose uniforms were faded but whose guns were bright."

Right: Buchanan took the "captain of the ship of state" metaphor literally, sailing toward the White House on this miniature of the *U.S.S. Constitution.* (Columbia Historical Society)

Below: Garfield's 1881 parade threaded this grandiose temporary arch, wrought from wood painted to imitate bronze. (Library of Congress)

Opposite: American Indian chiefs marched along with Roughriders in Theodore Roosevelt's 1905 parade. (Painting by Frank Wright; collection of Perpetual Savings Bank)

Inaugurals brought out a kind of rambunctious American splendor: Van Buren, in a carriage of oak pried from the hull of the frigate *Constitution*, set a precedent. "From that time to this," observed Collins in 1909, "the spectators at this free show would vote a parade a stupid affair did it not present some extraordinary sight." Of those, there was no dearth: Buchanan's Ship of State — on wheels; Theodore Roosevelt bully-well waving to the tune of "There'll Be a Hot Time in the Old Town Tonight"; "old-style Indians [TR's words] in their war paint" in the same parade; Warren G. Harding testing the first inaugural automobile ride; the Kennedy reviewing stand, called by D.C. Republican Chairman Carl Shipley "the Hanging Gardens of Babylon"; Jimmy Carter's solar heating panels on his stand; Garfield's ride through not one but thirty-nine richly wrought, wooden Grand Arches — the grandest astride Fifteenth Street. Less than a year later, the Avenue would be lined with tanbark, and the Pennsylvania Railroad would build a branch track to the very edge of the Avenue, to make his ride easier as the mortally wounded president was carried to the same railroad station where he'd been shot.

Be Prepared was a wise inaugural maxim. Unscramble the floats, round up the piccolo player, hang the bunting, hire the shovel-and-bucket brigade. And see to the bird-proofing. "The last time we bird-proofed the stands," D.C. Buildings and Grounds Director James Blaser told the *Washington Daily News* in 1965, "everybody got the message but the birds." Best get the overhead sheeting up a day early.

Right: Prelude to national mourning. Lincoln's body is delivered from Peterson House to the White House via F Street. Later, on Pennsylvania Avenue, a funeral cortege delivered the bodies of the president and his son Willie, who had died three years earlier and was exhumed after his father's assassination, to the railroad station to begin the slow ride to Springfield, Illinois. "Despite the enormous crowd, the silence was profound." (National Archives)

Below: The dream is over: Kennedy's funeral made even more depressing by a tattered Avenue the president had vowed to clean up. (John F. Kennedy Library)

Opposite: Mourners across from the White House during FDR's funeral procession, April 14, 1945. (National Archives)

Above: Not all processions were grand and glorious. "Be Kind to Animals Week" of 1920 provided a bit of post-war whimsy, while this Ku Klux Klan march of 1926 *(right)* wasn't exactly a source of national pride. (Library of Congress and Columbia Historical Society)

Left: It wasn't the year of a Republican inauguration. Simply a 1907 circus parade passing up the Avenue at Twelfth Street. (Columbia Historical Society)

There is something about broad Pennsylvania Avenue that brings out a parade. In 1871, when they spent two million dollars to pave it with wood blocks, sweeping it as clean as a parlor floor, Washington went wild. Chinese lanterns, goat races, strong drink at Newkirk's and Beveridge's saloons — and the darndest marchers the town had ever seen — threw an impetuous street carnival. The toot began, John Clagett Proctor reported, with the search for "broken down horses for the use of those drafted as commanding officers. Old smokestacks were impressed for cannon, and ... whitewash brushes and Potomac herrings were used for epaulets, and old brooms and broom handles supplied the arms. A Mr. Nathan Edmonston, said to have had a harelip and extremely hard to understand, was elected by the revelers as general." Good times rolled in 1889, as well, for the "wheelmen's lantern parade." "A Fairy Scene on Pennsylvania Avenue Last Night," the *Evening Star* reported. Some of the impatient cyclists, including

those of Tricycle Division No. 9, lit their candles early and, "like the improvident maidens who were waiting for the Biblical bridegroom, came to grief before the affair was over, as their dips began to sputter and they gasped out, leaving them in darkness." Benjamin Harrison poked his head out of the White House to see what the fuss was about.

The nation's ceremonial way would capture the spirit of America's freedom of petition and assembly, in the march of women's suffragists in 1913 and of klansmen in '25. They took a historic cue from a string of protests and celebrations that had been drawn to the Avenue like deer to a salt lick. Jacob Coxey and his "march of living petition" by what he called the "Commonweal of Christ" from Massillon, Ohio, passed by in 1894; he was jailed, but sympathetic "industrial armies," stealing trains and otherwise scrambling, arrived to support him. Their zeal was slaked when the District of Columbia government agreed to pay their way home, and they quickly dispersed.

Two days of huzzahs greeted Admiral George Dewey, the hero of Manila Bay, and other Spanish-American War vets in 1899. In 1916, President Wilson, an American flag hoisted on his shoulder, marched in a Preparedness Day parade. Spontaneous marchers banging tin pans and washtubs marked Armistice Night in 1918, as three hundred thousand deleriants looked on. A latter-day Avenue arch, modeled after the *Arc de Triomphe*, welcomed Black Jack Pershing, astride his thoroughbred Jeff, and more than twenty-five thousand survivors of the Great War in 1919. "Only 12 drunks were arrested," the *Star Magazine* reported. "Prohibition might have had something to do with it." President Harding and former President Taft, together with other world leaders, walked behind the funeral cortege of the Unknown Soldier in 1921. An infirm former President Wilson followed in a carriage. Washington's chance to shower aviator Charles A. Lindbergh, not with ticker tape, but more likely with shreds of government ledgers, came in 1927. In 1932, some fifteen thousand World War I veterans, who had been promised a service bonus to be paid in 1945, descended upon Washington, demanding that the payment be moved up. This Bonus Army marched down the Avenue to lobby the Senate (the House having acquiesced), but that body and President Hoover turned down the idea as too expensive. Tanks, at the command of General Douglas MacArthur, with Major Dwight D. Eisenhower at his side, routed Bonus Expeditionary Force marchers from the Avenue and Bonus Army squatters from abandoned buildings set for demolition in the Federal Triangle in 1932.

One of the Avenue's gentlest processions, on a snowy January afternoon in 1883, was recalled by L. R. Grabill in a letter to his sister: It was an impromptu sleighing carnival, with prizes for the most original, and most grotesque, rigs and masks. Grabill wasted little space on the first-place sled, a take-off on a London hansom. "The second prize was a 'Court,'" he wrote.

A cow hauled on a sled with Mrs. Langtry as Defendant holding her horns and the Plaintiff pulling her tail, while the counsel on both sides milked her. That cow must have got milked dry before the procession was done. The third prize was taken by an old lady with an old-fashioned green split-bottomed rocking chair for a sleigh, with a horse hitched to the front pulling it. The chair, not being well balanced, jerked and rocked about a good deal, and the fellow in it surely earned his prize [during his four-mile ride].

The tintinabulation of the bells from 300 to 400 sleighs, Grabill closed, "makes my ears ring yet."

Above: This music store near Twelfth Street was the former headquarters of the Christian Heurich Brewery and of the Admiral Dewey Reception Committee, which feted the hero of Manila Bay ("You may fire when you are ready, Gridley") with an Avenue parade in 1899. (Washingtoniana Division, D.C. Public Library)

Above right: When General John J. Pershing came marching home from the Great War, the nation honored him and twenty-five thousand soldiers with this temporary Arc de Triomphe in 1919. Reported one newspaper: "Only 12 drunks were arrested. Prohibition might have had something to do with it." (Columbia Historical Society)

Right: Three years after he carried a flag in a Preparedness Day march, President Wilson led a welcome home parade in 1919. The Willard, Raleigh, and Occidental hotels were all preening in their prime. (Library of Congress)

Opposite top: The Bonus March parade of July 28, 1932, was another nadir. Veterans who were seeking benefits they thought due them, this ragtag brigade was routed by tear gas and Douglas MacArthur in 1932. Two vets were killed and about fifty injured. (Acme Newsphoto, National Archives)

Above: FDR's first inauguration was as old-fashioned as a mustache cup, but his third on January 20, 1941, was all tanks and business. This carefully researched painting by Washington artist Frank Wright depicts what was intended to be a show of preparedness. Marching are color-bearers from the four branches of the armed services. They're wearing their combat uniforms, not parade dress. In the photo *(opposite bottom),* also a 1941 scene, note at left the old Ford auto plant, where the first Model A was introduced. (Painting by Frank Wright, photo from Washingtoniana Division, D.C. Public Library)

99

Carter eschewed the limousines and tanks of years past to stroll the Avenue. Recalled Rosalynn Carter, it was so cold that the lips of band members froze to their reeds. (Jimmy Carter Library)

Everyone of any tooth in Washington has an Avenue snow or winter story of streetcars lined nose-to-tail, clear to Georgetown. Rosalynn Carter, in her autobiography, had one from her husband's inaugural parade. So cold was the day, Mrs. Carter wrote, that the lips of some band members froze to their reeds. Another tale, from Washingtonian Louis G. Buttell, is of "the night before the Kennedy inauguration," when "it snowed like crazy."

It wasn't the depth, so much; I think it was just 7.7 inches. But it fell in a short time and seemed like a lot more. It tied the city in knots. People trying to get to preinaugural parties were trapped in their cars for hours, and many never got there at all. National Airport was snowed in, and many inaugural visitors were unable to get here. It created a bonanza for most hotels, which had required nonrefundable payments on rooms of four days. So when the snow stranded thousands of people at home, the hotels turned around and resold the rooms to people looking desperately for a place to get in from the snow.

I recall leaving my office at around 4:30 p.m. to catch a trolley car up to our apartment at Sixteenth and Irving. But because salt had shorted out the electrical lines powering the trolleys — at least that's what the newspapers said [more likely it was hunks of broken automobile chains, jammed in the third-rail slot] — my line to Columbia Road in Mount Pleasant was backed up to Pennsylvania Avenue. I walked a good ways home. That night I was to touch base with people from New York who were bringing in the March of Dimes poster girl for the inaugural parade. My wife and I walked to their hotel and found that they were some of the lucky ones who made it in and found rooms.

As usually happens, the next day dawned bright, clear, and bitterly cold. They'd called out the army to shovel the Avenue all night to get it ready. Due to some bureaucratic snafu, someone gave the signal for the floats to leave their underground staging area, under the Capitol, about two hours too early. I was waiting at the other end of the Avenue to catch the March of Dimes girl and other children in costume— I'd lined up Cinderella in a skimpy little fairy outfit. They sat outside, in the freezing cold, for hours before moving onto the parade route. It's a wonder those poor kids didn't get frostbite. I think their parents slipped them jackets and some cocoa; the adults along the route were into something a little stronger. But those kids were troopers. When the float came past, there they were, waving and trying to keep their teeth from chattering when they smiled.

THE ERA OF
RECONSTRUCTION

Monumental Undertakings

A merica's nonpareil architects, sculptors, and landscape architects created a glittering fairyland at the 1893 World's Columbian Exposition in Chicago. The Great White City of temporary buildings "was stamped on the memory of the whole nation," wrote Fiske Kimball in *American Architecture* magazine. Inspired visitors went home to gritty cities, rhapsodizing about a vision realized of a City Beautiful. When the American Institute of Architects was invited to convene in Washington in 1900 to mark the capital's centennial, the architects were asked to present papers on the unrequited plans of Major L'Enfant. At President McKinley's behest, they met with high government officials, James McMillan of Michigan, chairman of the Senate Committee on the District of Columbia, among them. He asked the visitors to help conceptually untangle the city's Great Mall. Pleased at their enthusiasm, McMillan pushed through a bill authorizing his committee to employ experts to address the region's splayed network of parks. The consultants, whom this scion of Grosse Point eventually had to pay himself, became known as the Senate Park—or McMillan—Commission, and its pale soon spread far beyond trees and brooks.

The senator and his secretary, Charles Moore, appointed the impresario of the Chicago Fair, Daniel Burnham, as commission chair. Landscape architect Frederick Law "Little Rick" Olmsted, Jr., designer of the Boston park system, and architect Charles McKim, a classicist who had studied at École des Beaux-Arts in Paris, soon joined him, and the members together recruited another World's Fair compatriot, sculptor Augustus Saint-Gaudens. The commission's charge: to build "a work of civic art" in a capital city "worthy of the nation."

Senate Park commissioners then set sail on a regal, seven-week inspection tour of Europe and the Middle East, basking in Greco-Roman precedent. The "thought of the strength, power, and mastery of imperial Rome" made Burnham "walk erect," wrote Moore, the commission's note taker. The group's final report, released at an extravagant exhibit blessed by President Theodore Roosevelt, featured McKim's intricate scale models of the city as it appeared and as they fantasized it. The plan proposed a Lincoln Memorial and a stately bridge to

Pages 102–103: A contemporary, aerial view of Pennsylvania Avenue, viewed from the Capitol looking toward the White House. (Carol M. Highsmith)

Opposite top: Senator James McMillan of Michigan. His mission to analyze the region's parks spawned a commission that would try to remake the Avenue as one long, gleaming temple. (PADC)

Opposite bottom: Daniel H. Burnham, the architect-tycoon who envisioned a neoclassical future for the Avenue. The "thought of the strength, power, and mastery of imperial Rome [made him] walk erect." (PADC)

Above: There may not have been enough travertine in the world to execute this magniloquent 1902 vision of the Avenue and the Mall. (PADC)

Arlington Cemetery, but it virtually ignored the city's commercial core. "It was along Pennsylvania Avenue that the McMillan Plan was least successful," the President's Council on Pennsylvania Avenue would report sixty-three years later. "From having been a great urban bond [between federal and local interests], Pennsylvania Avenue was in fact reduced to being the boundary between the two." Pumped by the promotional contrivances of Moore, who spoon-fed stories to the press, and by the AIA secretary Glenn Brown's rousing speeches to civic groups as far away as St. Louis, the commission rode a City Beautiful steamroller of public favor, taking pains to downplay the newness of their schemes in favor of heroic references to L'Enfant and the wistful past. Masterful PR or no, the bitter opposition of House Speaker Joseph Cannon, no patron of the arts, who was miffed that the House had been aced out of any glory, stymied adoption of the McMillan Plan. So did congressional ennui generally, since the plan added no more votes back home. But the grandiose remaking of official Washington, which had begun with Burnham's Union Station would take place in stages anyway.

Right: This aerial view avant-Triangle shows seventy acres of brothels and other low-life. (Washingtoniana Division, D.C. Public Library)

Below: Buildings the Federal Triangle uprooted housed saloons, clubs, shops, theaters — just the sort of life that was sorely missed on the Avenue in the sixties and seventies. (National Archives)

Opposite: More "unsightly places" along the Avenue, which was lined with gas stations, tattoo parlors, chop suey signs, and rooming houses. Said one observer, "The little shops with slovenly fronts . . . offend citizens with dignified ideas." (Washingtoniana Division, D.C. Public Library)

President William Howard Taft sought and received a bill creating a Fine Arts Commission, whose domain he soon extended to the approval of public buildings in the District of Columbia. Burnham was named its first chairman, and his friend and fellow grand-traveler, Moore, would later hold the post for twenty-two years. Moore was an unbridled classicist. With an appreciative bow to the Capitol, White House, and Treasury Department Building, he told the Washington Society of Fine Arts that Washington "was founded and is developed in an architectural fashion which belongs to the ages." The Fine Arts Commission became what Sally Kress Tompkins called "a closed club" of wealthy architects wielding withering influence in the capital city. Perish the thought, as Commissioner Cass Gilbert would write a friend, that "the head of a new or special department might be a cubist, a futurist or a Mullett." Alfred B. Mullett had designed what became the Old Executive Office Building, whose ornate "pseudo-classical style" drove Moore to decry the "chaos in the arts."

Further maneuvers led to the creation of a Public Buildings Commission, whose aim was to get government clerks out of scattered, high-cost, rented offices and into mighty new departmental buildings. Federal employment in the capital more than tripled between 1901 and 1926, when sixty-five thousand Washington bureaucrats were on the payroll. The buildings commission homed in on the sordid south side of Pennsylvania Avenue, which the Fine Arts Commission report of 1916-18 said "nothing short of radical measures" could save.

As early as 1891, plans had been advanced for leveling the blight and cutting two new avenues, National and Union, creating "a superb vista from the Capitol Dome to the colonnades of the [envisioned] Parthenonic Temples of the National Galleries" to the west. The government had already purchased the land that would become the base of a Federal Triangle, between Fourteenth and Fifteenth streets on the Avenue's south side.

In 1906, Senator Weldon B. Heyburn of Idaho had floated his own "Heyburn Plan" to condemn all private property between the Avenue and the Mall. Senator Knute Nelson of Minnesota ridiculed the idea that anything worthwhile could rise "in that low, swampy, and most disagreeable part of the city. . . . We all know that a good deal of this proposed purchase is a part of the slum of the city, and we know the rest is as unproductive and as undesirable property as can be found anywhere." Why waste taxpayers' money on such land, Nelson fretted. "Business has been for years drifting to the north and northwest, and in half a dozen years more, especially if the police in this city do their duty, a large share of the buildings south of the avenue will be vacant, and we ought to be able to get the property for a song."

World War I put everything on hold, but in 1923 the Public Buildings Commission called for an immediate purchase of land and the beginning of construction. President Harding and his cabinet concurred, writing of "a great park" to the south of the Avenue, "dotted here and there with magnificent buildings." A land-acquisition bill was signed by President Coolidge in 1926. According to Tompkins, "The disgraceful conditions along Pennsylvania Avenue acted as a stimulus to Congressional approval. The ceremonial avenue was lined with gas stations, tattoo parlors, chop suey signs, rooming houses, and cheap hotels. Ohio Avenue, which cut through the Triangle area, was lined with brothels." Another writer, Mildred Adams, sniffed about "the little shops with slovenly fronts that offend citizens with dignified ideas." By Christmas of 1928, the federal government had purchased the entire seventy acres of the Triangle.

Implementation of the largest public building project in American history fell to Treasury Secretary Mellon, who named a board of consulting architects. In 1929, Mellon commissioned a silent film on the history of Washington, with emphasis on the decline of the Federal Triangle area. The film, which he showed at a meeting of the U.S. Chamber of Commerce, switched between shots of the Avenue and glorious master-plan mock-ups. In truth, the neighborhoods shown as models of decay in the grainy, jerky old film looked tree-lined, alive with traffic — not disgraceful at all — and far more human than the bureaucratic canyon that replaced them. "The worst of it [which the film did not show] was down around Four-and-a-half Street, leading down to Fort Leslie McNair," noted Frederick Gutheim years later. "It was filled with girls on the prowl — and boys on the prowl."

"New-fangled notions in architecture will not be allowed to sway the character of the great monumental structures," the *Star* quoted Mellon as assuring Congress. His architects, who promptly swore allegiance to the classicist Washington wisdom, received minimal expenses going in but a plum coming out: commissions to design the great buildings. Openly borrowing from the Louvre in Paris, they agreed on a uniform design concept of imposing, buff-colored limestone structures with tile roofs, set amid vast courtyards, circles, and gardens. Early suggestions of a new municipal marketplace to replace the squalid Center Market were quietly slid into storage; no fishmongers would

mar their majestic design. Archibald Hopkins of the Committee of One Hundred, a booster group for the old McMillan Plan, floated an idea for the north side of the Avenue, then still prosperous, across from the Triangle's hypotenuse. He suggested that it be lined with "government hotels" to allow federal workers to live close to their jobs in what John W. Stepp, writing in the *Star*, would call "massive Greco-Roman ant-hills."

Jockeying among cabinet members for prime building placement continued right up to 1937, when President Franklin D. Roosevelt laid the cornerstone for the last monolith to be built. It was the Apex Building, housing the Federal Trade Commission, in the smallest top slice of the Triangle cut by Pennsylvania and Constitution avenues and Sixth Street. One building, John Russell Pope's National Archives at Eighth Street, broke the symmetry of wall-like facades along the Pennsylvania Avenue diagonal. A late-comer to the Mellon Board, Pope got, for his Archives, a cross-axis that preserved L'Enfant's plan of a square at the Avenue midpoint. Any hope of a view of the Washington Monument from the Avenue through this new Great Wall of Government was obliterated by architects who, urban-planning theorist Elbert Peets wrote in a scathing critique, "in the privacy of their drafting rooms [enjoy nothing so much] as cutting a leg off M. L'Enfant's trousers."

Opposite top: The Apex Building under construction. FDR laid the cornerstone. The building displaced a forlorn dream bungalow that somehow found its way onto the nation's parade route. (National Archives)

Opposite bottom: Treasury Secretary Andrew Mellon's Triangle, with its buff-colored buildings, tile roofs, and courtyards, borrowed openly from the Louvre. (Portrait by Oswald Birley, National Gallery of Art)

Above: A view of the Federal Triangle closing in on completion (at a cost of $125 million, not counting land acquisition) in 1936. Noted *The WPA Guide to Washington:* "Each weekday morning 30,000 workers leave their homes, converge on this area, and disappear into the monumental buildings. . . . the flood of humanity clogs all transportation systems." (PADC)

Opposite: Facade of the Post Office Department, one of the structures that obscures the view of monuments. Said one critic, Triangle planners were gleefully "cutting a leg off M. L'Enfant's trousers." Triangle defenders include J. Carter Brown of the National Gallery of Art, who said, "we have come to recognize that they don't hardly build 'em like that anymore." (Carol M. Highsmith)

Right: What is Past is Prologue, an allegorical sculpture by Robert Aitken (and carved by Italian-American artisans), stands in front of the National Archives, a building that replaced Center Market in the 1930s. The project demonstrated why the area was once called Marsh Market. Because of spongy soil, the government had to drive more than eighty-five hundred piles to a depth of twenty-one feet to create sure footing for the Archives. (Carol M. Highsmith)

Left: Though a bureaucratic canyon to some, the Triangle is not without its pleasures. One is *Man Controlling Trade,* the 1942 sculpture by Michael Lantz located at the Federal Trade Commission. Carved on site out of limestone, the sculpture is one of a pair. (Carol M. Highsmith)

111

Most Triangle buildings turned their back on the Avenue, preferring a view of the increasingly sylvan Mall to that of banks, hotels, and tarnished Victorian office buildings. Indeed the Triangle, self-absorbed, was oriented more inward—toward an L-shaped Grand Plaza and a circular plaza across Twelfth Street—than to a world outside. Within the buildings' honeycomb of halls, artisans built a great aquarium, exuberant murals, heroic sculptures, and a steel curtain to safeguard national treasures. Most of these would never be seen by a public that's been frightened away, first by the buildings' intimidating scale, then by the security gauntlet of the nervous 1980s.

The Triangle's Grand Plaza soon became anything but esteemed. Its fountain was quickly surrounded by parked cars, which, though evolving in style over sixty years, would prove stubborn to move. The President's Council on the Avenue would write in 1964 that the plaza needed to be "rescued from the primitive standard of civilization evidenced by its present use as a rubble-strewn parking lot, in which the Great Republic lets the fine Strauss Memorial Fountain be faced by wooden shacks."

While the Triangle project proved aptly timed, putting thousands of laborers to work at the depths of the Great Depression, the $125 million acquisition and building project eventually ran out of budgetary steam. Underground parking, demolition of the Old Post Office, and its replacement by a wing of the Internal Revenue Service Building were among its uncompleted pieces.

In one sense the Federal Triangle had seemed in perfect step with L'Enfant's orderly plan, but by packing a single government reservation, it was in fact far out of phase; L'Enfant had scattered important buildings around the city. Tidy monumentalism appealed to the times, however. J. Frederick Essary wrote in the *Saturday Evening Post* in 1929 that a new capital "to awaken the patriot's pride" was about to emerge "from the artistic illiteracy and hodgepodgery of Washington," notably a Pennsylvania Avenue that "in some

respects [is] the most famous thoroughfare on the continent, and in some respects the ugliest."

Razed to build the Triangle project were the arcane Southern Railway Building, Harvey's oyster house, a little brick building that had served as a temporary capitol after the British sacked Washington in 1814, old warehouses turned into greasy parking garages, the city's Emergency Hospital, fire-engine house No. 12, iron- and woodworking shops, Poli's Theater (called "as ugly outside as it is beautiful within" by reporter L. C. Speers), and the previously noted brothels, not to mention what Massachusetts Representative Charles L. Underhill called "Chinese dens which have been a worry to the police and others."

The most curious casualty was a building the *Post* in 1934 called the "Forgotten Bungalow." It was a brand-new, two-story "demonstration house," erected by the Washington Home Building League and opened June 6, 1933, on the sliver that would house the Apex Building. The bungalow, and a small garage, were instead found "as one of Washington's most pathetic tragedies . . . standing lugubriously amidst an accumulation of rum bottles, oil drums, boiler tanks [and] dirt piles," and hidden behind a tall, wooden fence. When Mellon's wrecking crews sought to call the League to tell it to come get its house, they found the phone disconnected. So, said the *Post*, until the bulldozers arrived, the little house stood "like a lost orphan in thick traffic, cling[ing] bravely to a site."

Many critics at that time and later would deride the Triangle project. Peets called its stalwart design "a travesty" that "might make the Imperial Fora . . . the Louvre-Tuileries, and the Escorial look like Boy Scout stuff. But it won't. The Buildings Commission does not group its buildings; it parks them." Despite the preserve's uniformity, it showed poor planning, wrote Gutheim. "No anticipation of the needs of such a concentration of federal office workers had embraced the practical details of how they got to work, where they had lunch, or where they parked their cars." But J. Carter Brown, director of the National Gallery of Art just down the Avenue, would reflect later: "The Federal Triangle, which I have always loved and have felt was much maligned by a pendulum swing of architectural taste that decried ornamentation and classical illusion at a certain moment in the throes of beaux-arts enthusiasm, was considered a rather ludicrous anachronism. Maybe the pendulum swings too far the other way, but we have come more and more to recognize that they don't hardly build 'em like that anymore."

Opposite: The "grand plaza" envisioned for the Federal Triangle was by 1937 lost to commuter parking. (Washingtoniana Division, D.C. Public Library)

Above: Saved from leveling, the Old Post Office facade makes a bracing contrast with the Triangle's classicism. (Carol M. Highsmith)

Above: Around 1960, this old bank building at Tenth Street received a lethal dose of plate glass and heavy drapes. (James M. Goode Collection, Library of Congress)

Right: In the fifties and sixties, no one wanted to come to the Avenue to park, shop, or stroll. (National Archives)

Opposite: A Poor People's March comprising eleven mule-drawn wagons passes the Avenue on June 25, 1966. Within two years the smoldering ruins of Fourteenth Street would be visible from the Avenue. (AP Wirephoto)

114

O Lost! And By the Wind Grieved!

When the British burned the heart of Washington in 1814, "urban blight was so far advanced that many residents regarded the national embarrassment as a local blessing," wrote John D. Weaver in a 1968 *Holiday* magazine story. By the time John Kennedy rode up the Avenue in 1961, Weaver observed, "it seemed a good time to ask the British back." And this was a travel piece.

It had always been the sodden south side of the Avenue, with its bilious swamp and nefarious neighborhoods that, as Archibald Hopkins recounted, had been "an eyesore unworthy of being the principal street of a third-rate, backward town." "If you venture on the south side of the Avenue, watch your purse," warned an 1850s guidebook. In its ham-handed way, the Federal Triangle fixed that. Soon it was the Avenue's north side that, like much of inner-city America, became tattered as every source of urban nourishment hied to the suburbs and glitzy uptown strips. The Avenue looked so shabby that, in 1964, Carl Shipley suggested moving the inaugural route to Constitution Avenue. "Of course there are glaring esthetic deficiencies along the Avenue and its northern environs," replied the *Star*, "and they should be corrected. The way to accomplish that necessary goal, however, is to face the problems — not to run away from them."

"The fifties and sixties were a time when cities pushed the panic button," noted D.C. planner John Fondersmith. It was a time of free-swinging wrecker's balls, squiggly overlays on city highway maps, and mastodonic buildings and leviathan squares. Cities are like gardens, and buildings are like plants, the reasoning went. Weeds grow. Plants die. So you dig up the garden, sprinkle on some federal fertilizer, and start over.

The Willard Hotel closed in 1968. "You could tell the end was near," remembered Washington architect Hugh Newell Jacobsen, "when out went the marble and in came the formica, and when the waitresses had corsages made out of napkins and asked you, 'What can I get you, hon?'"

It was in the same year that riots followed the assassination of Martin Luther King, Jr., striking fear in the heart of a city and driving a stake to the gut of downtown. In *10 Blocks From the White House*, Ben Gilbert, then *Washington Post* managing editor, would describe the frenetic looting, wanton arson, and braggadocio taunting of terrified commuters. Twenty years later, from his home in Tacoma, Washington, he would point out, "There's a photograph in the book, showing armed soldiers in the lee of the Capitol. They were protecting the seat of government. When you send troops to occupy the Capitol, the symbolism of the fact that the Avenue was *not* closed down meant that the government of the United States continued." Roving bands of youths, some raging, some mirthful, pillaged almost at will. D. J. Kaufman's, a high-fashion men's shop just off the Avenue at Tenth Street, took a hit, but the real devastation was along Seventh and Fourteenth streets. "After the 'civil disturbances,'" remembered F Street shoestore owner Frank H. Rich, "business completely dropped dead" — for the Avenue as well as for him.

Above: Kann's department store at Seventh Street declined after the 1968 riots. Efforts to spruce up the old buildings with metal panels failed. In 1979 the paneling was pried off, revealing an intact and potentially reusable building beneath. But within days, Kann's was scorched for good. (PADC)

Opposite: Austin Kiplinger, president and CEO of Kiplinger Washington Editors. (Carol M. Highsmith)

"All of the people that were landlords basically said there is no reason to put any money into these buildings, to refurbish them," recalled Stephen L. Davidson, who took over Apex Liquors from his father in 1972 and sold the building to PADC in 1981. "They knew at some point these blocks could or would be eliminated, so the buildings began to really deteriorate. There was nothing ever done to brighten them up or make them better. The riots were really the impetus. The owners were scared that they'd go ahead and refurbish, and the same thing could happen next year."

Construction, in dully utilitarian eggcrate fashion, of the Pennsylvania Building at Thirteenth Street and the Avenue in 1953 was the last foursquare effort to stanch the economic bleeding downtown. Kann's, in business since 1886, had put together as many as fifteen tiny buildings to make its store at Market Space. Kann's was a bustling fixture, especially during the holidays, when Christmas windows would be unveiled for hundreds of little noses to press against. Toy trains, jolly figurines, and tiny cars pulled 'round by unseen chains have given way to simpler delights, spread along the Avenue. But by 1959 Kann's was hanging on with a strictly déclassé new customer base. It tried to look presentable by slapping on aluminum siding. "The old clientele moved or died out," said Vice President B. Bernei Burgunder, Jr. In 1975, Kann's gave up and closed; it stood empty, an aluminum eyesore, for four years before a suspicious fire gutted the building and it was demolished. A similar shopping institution, Lansburgh's, just up Seventh Street, had been closed since 1973.

Article after article depicted the decay that soon saturated the Avenue, like termites devouring a rotting stump. "Grubby," one called the auction houses, incoherent winos, and peep stalls that lined the soiled boulevard. "The only reason there weren't X-rated theaters," recalled Elwood "Pete" Quesada, who would later chair a commission to revitalize the Avenue, "was that they couldn't draw any nighttime business. Not even perverts would go there." His executive director at PADC, John Woodbridge, recalled his first full encounter with the Avenue in 1963. "It convinced me that Washington was a city with southern efficiency and northern charm." The only reason 90 percent of the buildings were still standing, he later wrote the *Star*, was that "the area is economically dead," and no one would invest in rebuilding it. Pitching for the incipient PADC plan, he added, "If we are too cheap to attempt a [sweeping] solution that has some visual harmony with the tradition of Washington, then we should prepare ourselves to sit in the present squalor and await the inevitable economic strangulation."

Remembered Charles Horsky, adviser on District of Columbia affairs to both presidents Kennedy and Johnson, "I understand why someone who thought of the Avenue as the Main Street of the United States would be disappointed. There were buildings with souvenirs on the bottom floors, then three or four floors of plywood [-covered windows]. You'd say, Jesus Christ, this is Pennsylvania Avenue?" On the site of the spanking-bright 1201 Pennsylvania Avenue office building in which his law office would later locate, he recalled, stood "a crummy little garage. There were maybe a couple of cheap restaurants, but otherwise no reason to come down here." As late as 1977, when Andy Barnes moved to Washington as a White House fellow, he found "the north side of the Avenue depressing. I'd heard marvelous stories about an avenue much alive. I could picture Mathew Brady in his studio. It was tough [a year later, when he joined PADC] to walk up and down those streets, taking inventory, seeing boarded-up buildings, down-and-out street people hanging out on corners, the National Theatre struggling, the Press Club on hard times." By then, he said, "banks were red-lining the area."

When the PADC first approached Congress for funding in the early 1970s, Senator Alan Bible of Nevada asked officials for some figures. He got them: a 42 percent loss of business in the Pennsylvania Avenue corridor between 1960 and 1969. Ten totally vacant buildings, 82 vacant above the first floor. Among the 177 firms still in business, the redevelopment corporation counted 6 bars, a bed-

ding outlet, a burlesque house, 6 coffee shops, 3 fireworks stands, 6 discount stores, 12 hat or wig shops, 6 liquor stores, 3 palm readers, 7 porno shops, and one diehard religious organization.

An obvious question — How could the Capital of the Free World let itself go to seed? — was answered by retired Fine Arts Chairman William Walton. "Pennsylvania Avenue never caught the imagination," he said. "It always had to be pushed. The White House had its agenda, and Congress was always more interested in the top of the Hill."

Austin Kiplinger, president and CEO of the Kiplinger Washington Editors, noted that "nobody in the federal government has paid consistent, close attention to the city; it's been an orphan."

Often there is nobody at the White House with major responsibilities for coordination with the nation's capital, and Washington has had to improvise. Every once in awhile, a president or first lady picks a particular project, as in Mrs. Johnson's interest in beautification, which helps the city. Then that incumbent leaves the White House, and those who fight the good fight for Washington have to start over; there's no continuity.

Planning for this nation's capital, in particular, is a hodgepodge. Counties, two states, the District and federal governments, independent towns and cities, all have to have their say. The Council of Governments is just an advisory group. It's still popular in political campaigns to run *against* Washington. That attitude about the political seat of power gets confused with feelings about the city of Washington, so the city gets short shrift. Considering all that, it's a miracle that dramatic change for good, such as the handsome Pennsylvania Avenue redevelopment, ever gets accomplished. I guess necessity is a great motivator. It's a good thing, because Pennsylvania Avenue is a showcase for the country. It's the nation's front window.

Marvelous character — and characters — could be seen through it. A legend among early strollers was Beau Hickman, a regular at Hancock's Old English Inn and Antique Museum and other saloons in the "island" south of the Avenue. Beau had no visible means of support nor a coin to pay for drinks. Yet, observed a writer of his day, "He maintained himself as a fashion plate and dined and drank at the best places. He appeared uninvited at the most exclusive social functions and apparently was never thrown out by angry hosts." Once, this artful sponger took a train to Baltimore without benefit of ticket. He cut a piece of pasteboard in the form of a stub and found a seat near an open window. When the conductor approached, Beau carelessly brushed the "ticket" into the breeze. With a wish for an enjoyable journey, the conductor moved on.

117

A century later, Avenue fixtures included a demonstrative Irish cop, Ray Taylor, who directed traffic at Fourteenth and Penn — harking back to the days when hand-turned semaphores, not lights, signaled stop and go — and a sandwich chef named Barney Susser, who delighted customers at his deli at 621 Pennsylvania Avenue with a 1950s version of a Don Rickles insult routine.

Six storytellers, all of whom touched the Avenue, picked out others in a passing parade of the unorthodox:

Al Wise, who came to Washington from Boston in 1929 to work as a busboy at the Hotel Washington. He later rose to captain and head waiter:

The John McCormacks came in from Massachusetts to speak. She wanted her windows washed, but she wanted them washed from the outside, so the only thing we could do was, when she was out, go in and clean them from the inside and tell her the job was done. When John McCormack became speaker, Mrs. McCormack would come down, and every afternoon at three o'clock I had to bring her dog an order of American cheese.

Fanny Brice stayed with us. She was the last of the Ziegfeld Follies. I brought her breakfast and told her how I liked the show at the National Theatre. She was very pleased. She was a very tall woman, and her bed wasn't long enough. You could see her feet sticking out on the end.

With the first check Melvyn Douglas got [also at the National], he went down to Raleigh's and bought some

clothes. I came in in the morning with his breakfast, and I'd see his underwear hanging up. One of the most popular actors in the United States, and he washed his underwear himself.

Einstein's secretary, nobody wanted to wait on him. He was a coffee fiend. So I said, "Give him to me." I got him up to 75 cents [tip]. The other guys couldn't believe it. The politicians tipped the worst. They wanted a pat on the back.

One of the guests was the president of Schlitz Beer. I only met him once, but he used to send me a case of Schlitz every week. I didn't drink beer, but one of the German waiters really enjoyed the stuff.

One time the [John Nance] Garners had to give a dinner for the President. When he got off the elevator, Jimmy [Roosevelt, FDR's son] was holding up one arm, and the head of the Secret Service was holding up the other. They got out of the elevator and went into the front room, where we had drinks ready for them. We had a table set up for dinner. Behind the centerpiece, Franklin would have his two martinis where nobody could see it.

David Krupsaw, who owned The Sleep Center at 807 Pennsylvania Avenue from 1937 to 1980:

I was walking toward Eighth Street, and there was three dollars sitting on the sidewalk that people just passed by. I picked up the three dollars, and I still have them. I carry them in my wallet — have since the 1960s. And I've been very lucky!

When I got out of the service, I went down to Goozh's Gifts [815 Pennsylvania] one day. They wanted to know if I was interested in a blind date, and I said "Yeah." It turned out to be Jean, who I'd met many years ago in high school. Three months after seeing her again at Goozh's shop, we were engaged, and three months later, we were married.

Fred Litwin, owner of Litwin Furniture, half a block off Pennsylvania Avenue on Indiana Avenue:

A man comes in here in the '70s with a black homburg and an umbrella. I remember it so clearly because I felt like such an ass afterward. He said, "Hi, Fred, I need a china closet," and he looked familiar. I thought, "He knows my name?" I showed him the china closet, and I asked him why he needed it, as if it was any of my business. He said, "When the fellows come down, we serve tea. I have to go upstairs to get teacups, and I'd like to have them in the office." We talked back and forth. He didn't get the china closet. At the end of the conversation, I told him, "I feel crazy. You look familiar, but I don't know who you are, and you obviously know who I am." He said, "Well, my name is Burger." Burger! Warren Burger, the chief Supreme Court justice! He knows *me*, and I don't know him. I mean, you feel like a jerk!

A man comes in with a woman, and he was looking for a coffee table. He had a real German accent. It was the German that you'd hear in Berlin, very classy and a little high-pitched. He was short, and he was good-looking. While we were walking around I said, "You know, you sound like Wernher

Von Braun," and he stopped and he said, "*I am* Wernher Von Braun!"

Barney's is where I ate. Every day, I would eat a pastrami sandwich. At breakfast I would go in and get the worst cup of coffee you could get in the city. I went because that's where the humor and the fun was.

Nineteen-sixty-eight. That was the May Day demonstration. It was astonishing! Here, at the circle, there were a lot of young people that were going to stop the city, shut it down, stop government from operating. They said they were "impacting" it. The police were being flimflammed and whipsawed back and forth. The people that were called "youth" were really very strapping, powerful people. Cars were being pushed over in the intersection, and I'm not used to seeing that kind of violence. One on one, they were all right, but not very coherent. A woman was driving north on Seventh Street, slowly came into the intersection, and a young man, college student, six foot, heavy boots, fatigues. . . . This guy *ran* into the intersection, onto the hood of the car, and with the heel of his boot he smashed the windshield, right in the face of the woman. I went to the corner and looked up, and I saw police rounding up people who were just going to work. The police sat them against the wall, and a big paddy wagon came and poured them all in and took them away.

Opposite: Al Wise, former head waiter of the Hotel Washington: "When John McCormack became Speaker, Mrs. McCormack would come down, and every afternoon at three o'clock I had to bring her dog an order of American cheese." He also recalled serving Melvyn Douglas and Fanny Brice, who were performing at the National Theatre. (Carol M. Highsmith)

Above: In the wake of the streetcar era, the Avenue was cut up into new auto lanes and pedestrian islands, as demonstrated in this 1970 view taken near the National Theatre. (Paul M. Schmick, Washington Star Collection, D.C. Public Library)

Above: The early 1970s brought more fracas than festivity to the Avenue. Here a group of clergy and laypeople from Philadelphia lie on the sidewalk in front of the White House to protest U.S. bombing of Indochina. The sign reads "300 more today killed in Indochina by U.S. bombs." (AP Wirephoto)

Opposite: Al Cohen of Al's Magic Shop, a onetime Avenue fixture: "When the Second World War was over, I got off a train from Atlantic City, and we heard the guns going off. We got to Union Station, and you couldn't walk. It was thousands of people. I got to the store. It was solid people all the way. Very happy people." (Carol M. Highsmith)

Mark Weiss, who bought the camera department of The Timekeepers watch-repair shop on Pennsylvania Avenue, then opened two other camera stores under his own name on the Avenue:

The parades were something. It was hard to move on Pennsylvania Avenue when you had a parade. If somebody was short, they'd let them go in front to see what was going on. Everybody was very friendly. You didn't see fights.

Stephen L. Davidson, whose father turned a drugstore's small liquor department into Apex Liquors at 633 Pennsylvania Avenue. The store made ten thousand dollars during its first week in 1954, thirty thousand the second. The building, once the workplace of photographer Mathew Brady, was sold to PADC in 1981:

There were a lot of Damon Runyon–type characters on the Avenue. In the block between Sixth and Seventh there were two major bookie operations. Barney [of Barney's deli] was an ex-bookmaker, an ex-performer. He would insult federal judges, Supreme Court judges, anybody who walked in there. Steve's Cafe was famous because Steve was a bookmaker. He died in Barney's; he had a heart attack. You'd go in there and get a good meal and place a bet. You would see a lot of famous lawyers in there all during the day, playing dollar poker. The Avenue Souvenir Shop was an out-and-out bookmaking operation. They used to hate it when people would come in and buy souvenirs! Next to Barney's, you had a poolroom which attracted the most interesting people in Washington, a lot of ex-fighters, prize fighters, gangsters. You could place a bet with guys who sat [outside, on the Avenue] on cane-back chairs. The street was lined with sycamore trees, and they would sit under the trees. Nobody, including the police, would bother them.

At Seventh and Pennsylvania Avenue, there was a guy who sold newspapers, a fellow named Whitey. He sold what they called "dream books." If you had dreams, the dreams would correspond to numbers. If you dreamed about your boyfriend, that would be 8-0-3 or something. People would play these numbers.

We had a guy who came into our store and ran out with a couple of bottles. I had a crazy manager who ran after him and started shooting at the guy, *right on Pennsylvania Avenue!*

Lyndon Johnson was cheap, extremely cheap. We once had a sale on some liquor that we were losing about twenty cents a bottle on. He came walking into the store, and he wanted a case of it. We were limiting the people to six bottles. He wanted twelve bottles, and we only gave him six. So he walked out, got in the car, and sent his chauffeur in to get the other six bottles.

[John F.] Kennedy would come in from time to time. His brother [Robert] would come in more than he would. When he [Robert] was attorney general of the United States, he called me up and wanted a huge order. They were having some kind of party at the Justice Department. I had to remind him that it was illegal for us to deliver liquor into a government building.

There was a brand of liquor we were introducing called Hereford Cow. They tasted like milkshakes, but they had liquor in them. I called a cow farmer up in Gaithersburg, and he brought this cow down. We tied the cow up to the light post on Pennsylvania Avenue, put a big cowbell on it, and people came and took pictures.

May Day, there were so many people on the Avenue, it was a sea of humanity . . . so many people doing drugs at one time. There were hundreds of kids right in front of my store, passing bongs and pipes and smoking joints. I didn't see any violence, just lots and lots of drugs, sex, and rock 'n' roll. Girls were running around bare-breasted. It was quite a scene, and nobody was doing anything about it.

Al Cohen, whose father opened a souvenir shop on the Avenue in 1936. Al worked at the store and turned it into Al's Magic Shop:

We had a visit from President Truman one time, with his entourage. That was his big thing, to take a walk. He was always very interested in businesses. He and the whole Secret Service came in the shop. He looked around, we chatted a few minutes, and he asked, "How's business?"

I remember when the Second World War was over. I got off a train from Atlantic City, and we heard the guns going off, and we knew *something* had happened. They announced that the war was over. We got to Union Station, and you couldn't walk. It was thousands of people. I got from Union Station to the store [at Twelfth and Penn]. It was solid people the whole way. *Very* happy people.

You know, when they closed us down, made us move, they talked about how the Avenue had declined. I didn't see any decline. It had been that way for years.

Others of higher station did, however, see and act upon the Avenue's slide into tawdriness. The telling of it calls forth a modern parable.

The nation's capital has slept in the lap of many legends. An enduring tale describes John F. Kennedy's scornful inspection of Pennsylvania Avenue on his inaugural ride. Having barely removed his top hat, he is said to have noted, with well-bred disdain, the tacky state into which the Avenue of Presidents had fallen, and to have barked, "It's a disgrace — fix it," or words to that effect.

In commanding the grand face-lift, the young president is even said to have quoted Pericles to his new secretary of labor, Arthur J. Goldberg: "We do not imitate. We set an example for others." Thus admonished, the story goes, agency heads scurried to produce the first comprehensive plan for revitalizing the forlorn old boulevard.

The tale is not apocrypha, insisted many of his

friends and aides-de-camp. "It was gospel among all of us that he said it, and I have no reason to doubt it," recalled Charles Horsky. "It *was* a crummy street, and he *did* ride up it." William Walton, initially Kennedy's informal arts adviser and one of his best friends, rode two cars ahead of the president in 1961.

In the slow progress, when you're out there alone in a car, you have time to look at [the surroundings]. It was funny how all of us in different cars commented how shabby the Avenue was. On the left side, there's a row of architecture that has a certain serenity and size and grandeur. The other side was a mishmash, three-story buildings to rather out-of-date skyscrapers. There were the liquor stores, but those were fine; they gave the Avenue life, which has got to be restored someday. We, the president included, wanted to upgrade it, but we had many, many arguments over how we could bring life to Pennsylvania Avenue.

But Austin Kiplinger, who has written extensively about Washington, said, "I mistrust these stories about how things started with one lightning bolt, one man looking out the window of his car during the inauguration. These are fanciful stories, fine for symbolic purposes, but they are usually not true, or so little true. Nothing like that catches on until conditions ripen, until people realize, almost by consensus, that the time has come when we have to do something."

But was it revisionist history that had put in the mind of a new president, flush from delivering a powerful inaugural address, powers of concentration so acute that he would tune out the cheers and waves of adoring crowds long enough to make a mental note to *do something* about Pennsylvania Avenue?

Perhaps.

Aside from brother Bobby, Arthur Goldberg was President Kennedy's closest friend in the cabinet. A distinguished Chicago labor lawyer who had come to Washington as general counsel of the CIO labor federation, Goldberg would become a fixture in JFK's "brain trust." Justice Goldberg, whom Kennedy appointed to the Supreme Court a year into his administration, set the record as he saw it. Seventy-nine and living in retirement on his Marshall, Virginia, farm, he allowed as how it was he, himself, along with another yeasty intellectual, Labor's executive assistant (later U.S. senator) Daniel Patrick Moynihan, who set the Avenue's reawakening in motion that day in January, more than two decades earlier.

"I don't think it hurts a great man to knock down a few legends," said Goldberg. "A president of the United States newly inaugurated has more important things to think about at that moment than the condition of Pennsylvania Avenue."

Along with other cabinet members, Goldberg was provided with an automobile in which to ride up Pennsylvania Avenue. "I was very much impressed with the day," he remembered, "and I was very much impressed with myself!

I was a new cabinet officer, the first time I had ever held public office. Riding in the car, I noticed vividly what I may have ignored as a Washingtonian since 1948: the dilapidated condition of this Avenue of the Presidents, which I then and now regard to be the most important thoroughfare in our nation's capital. At that time, it consisted of a bunch of decrepit pawn shops, taverns, horrible souvenir shops that took advantage of tourists, and second-hand clothing stores. In sum, it was a disgrace.

He filed, but never forgot, that impression.

The new secretary was soon dismayed to find the cabinet's smallest department scattered among fifteen buildings in and around town. Like other federal bureaucracies, Labor's work force had grown exponentially since the end of World War II. Goldberg was troubled both by its inefficiency and by its racial distribution: black clerical workers clustered downtown, white administrators closer to their homes in the suburbs.

At the next cabinet meeting [August 4, 1961], I raised with the president the problem of federal office buildings. Having served in World War II, I should have known: Never volunteer! Kennedy immediately said, "I agree with you, and will you chair a committee on government office space?" Well, I was stuck.

Goldberg said he then called in Moynihan, who shared the belief that a great refitting of the Avenue might be unobtrusively tucked into a plan to rejigger office space. Thus, under an ad hoc committee of thirty leading architects, whom Goldberg recruited and who worked *pro bono*, did it develop. Out of their discussions and Moynihan's final report, Justice Goldberg recalled, would spring ideas "for enhancing the beauty of the Avenue, getting rid of all those slummy buildings, improving the surrounding area, and restoring it to what it should be: the Avenue of Presidents."

Pericles was in fact invoked by the president, according to Moynihan; by Moynihan, according to Goldberg who offered: "President Kennedy was not noted for being a classical scholar!" However, the retired justice would add, "I have always believed, having served our government in four or five capacities, that the person who signs the bottom line is entitled to the credit. And it is to Kennedy's great credit that, having had this situation called to his attention, he approved the recommendation."

Arthur Goldberg said the Avenue would always be close to the hearts of Americans. "The parade up Pennsylvania Avenue is one of the great events in the lives of every citizen of our country," he said. "This is especially true as it reaches, symbolically, to tie together the branches of our government." A quarter century after he first called attention to the deplorable state of the great Avenue, Justice Goldberg would admit to being "proud, very proud" of his role. "I'm not a fellow who likes to boast," he would say, "but I like to boast about that."

Goldberg and Moynihan did indeed slip a chapter on Pennsylvania Avenue into the otherwise turgid 1962 report on federal office needs, explaining in a cover letter that "Pennsylvania Avenue today is a scene where we find imposing [south side] Government buildings unhappily contrasted with [north side] blight and decay." Moynihan closed with a sentence that would be the banner of three commissions over a quarter-century: "This combination of effort [by public and private forces] can result in a concourse which will be lively, friendly and inviting." The report itself emphasized: "Pennsylvania Avenue should be the great thoroughfare of the City of Washington. Instead, it remains a vast, unformed, cluttered expanse." You could not call the area a slum, Moynihan would expound in the

Washington Post, since "no one lived there." Years later, Moynihan reminisced, "it was a critical time. The city was trying to float out toward Connecticut and Wisconsin avenues, and the idea of putting up modern, nongovernment buildings on the Avenue seemed hopeless because, over a century and a half, the plots were owned by a thousand people [and estates] in a thousand places. The city was in trouble, and you were heading eventually toward leaving the Capitol isolated, or worse."

The president never specifically approved the idea of setting up a commission to get to the heart of the matter, nor did he disapprove of it. It was a rash, wholly unofficial ploy that Moynihan, Fritz Gutheim, and William Walton cooked up, secure in the president's friendship. Goldberg, by then a Supreme Court justice, had bowed out of the conspiracy. Despite high-profile press coverage and its own officious certifications, the "President's Council on Pennsylvania Avenue," according to Moynihan, "never had any basis at all in Presidential proclamation. The plan was sort of drawn in barrooms and on street corners and at lots of dinners at the Occidental. Once, after the President was assassinated, I tried to get some piece of paper out of the White House that said, 'You were a member of the President's Council on Pennsylvania Avenue' — a name we just made up. The White House chief clerk, a forbidding man, said, 'Under no circumstances. There was no presidential authorization for this body whatever, and that's that.'"

Imprimatur or no, and working for free, this rump committee, chaired by eminent San Francisco architect Nathaniel Owings, a founding partner of Skidmore, Owings & Merrill, set to work. The group immediately eschewed normal General Services Administration planning channels, Moynihan said, "because they were the people who brought you the FBI Building and because GSA was a procurement agency. It had no energy of any kind. To be head of GSA is not a job that people with big ideas go for." But, in spontaneous, ever-provocative meetings, big ideas were exactly what this contraband commission came up with. With great gusto, members reconfigured the greatest avenue in America, over and over again, on paper. Owings and the others had corralled some of the nation's most explosive architectural brainpower, including that of Paul Thiry, master of the Seattle World's Fair; Douglas Haskell, editor of *Architectural Forum*; and Chloethiel Woodard Smith, who orchestrated the wholesale renewal of southwest Washington, D.C. Indeed, an "urban renewal" mentality gripped the council's early deliberations.

Top: When President Kennedy encountered the Avenue during his 1961 inauguration, he was reported to have said, "It's a disgrace. Fix it." (John F. Kennedy Library)

Bottom: Of stores that remained on the Avenue in the sixties, many were wig shops, souvenir stands, or liquor stores. Said one merchant: "When they closed us down, made us move, they talked about how the Avenue had declined. I didn't see any decline. It had been that way for years." (James M. Goode Collection, Library of Congress)

It was a time such urban renewal held sway. "Many a discussion, we talked about a total new avenue," recalled Chloethiel Smith. "I knew that if we left it in the hands of government alone — the gradual process — nothing would get done." Owings, she said, "tended to dominate. Everybody was fond of him, and in many ways he had a lot of good ideas, but he sure got people upset." John Woodbridge, who would be brought in by Owings to draw up the final plan, said, "Nat had some frustration on the committee in that he was unable to move or shake them very much, in part because they were as eminent as he, and partly because most of them were more given to talk than action." Gutheim, Walton, and Minoru Yamasaki pushed for divvying a proposed new cultural center into three parts and placing them all on Pennsylvania Avenue. Under one scheme, the District Building was to become an opera house; but supporters of a single building, what became the Kennedy Center for the Performing Arts, in Washington's Foggy Bottom, beat them to both the punch and to the president's favor.

Owings's council poured out designs that smacked of *Fantasia*. "He had asked Roy Allen of the New York SOM office to collaborate with him on one design that involved razing the entire north side

of the Avenue up to E Street, replacing it with a green park in which two skyscrapers of undetermined height would be built," recollected Woodbridge. "Thiry's plan also razed the north side and replaced it with a great podium, under which were parking and circulation, and above which were a series of futuristic, triangular-shaped buildings." Landscape architect Dan Kiley

had predictably planted a great boulevard of trees on the north side. This perhaps is the most enduring piece of the design of these early efforts, since there is a row of trees. William Turnbull, then a junior SOM designer, made the first drawing of the National Square. I can remember vividly when we pinned it on the end of the Avenue, like the tail on the donkey. Owings got up and said, "That's it." We spent the rest of the steamy Washington summer working days, nights, weekends, producing the drawings and the model for President Kennedy that fall.

The council once worked, Chloethiel Smith remembered, for forty-two hours straight, in what the *Post* later called "lofty isolation" from most city officials, scrubbing out buildings and reordering traffic patterns with the stroke of a stylus. At one point Owings asked members to go home and let their imaginations run wild, and to bring back plans from which the best elements might be drawn. "I took the challenge rather seriously," remembered Paul Thiry many years later. "I did a lot of work, put in a lot of thought. Ralph Walker put together a booklet, mostly of photographs of Paris and the great cities of the world. Yamasaki's plan was all green, green grass, white buildings, and more green grass. It precluded building up to Pennsylvania Avenue. When we didn't go along with his thinking, he got mad and quit."

Their distilled drawings produced the gargantuan National Square, a solid wall of new buildings along the Avenue's north side, and a spaghetti plate of underground freeways. "I don't think anyone who looked at these detailed, fantastic designs ever expected that they would be taken out and built that way," said Fritz Gutheim, "but they did establish the point that if we wanted development of the area as a whole, something of this sort had to come about."

In November 1963, a model was leaked to the press, drawing front-page attention in the *New York Times* — and the council's Green Book was made ready for President Kennedy's return from a trip to Dallas. The shocking news of the president's assassination temporarily knocked plans for Pennsylvania Avenue into a cocked hat. But after a period of mourning and cursing of Fate, they hitched their fortunes to a new president.

Opposite: Nathaniel Owings: Critics suggested he was spending too much time in temperate California and not enough striding along the summer broiler of the Avenue. "You could have a room full of forty people, senators, the president of the United States, and when that brawny man with the big hands would walk in . . . he was the center of the room in no time, irritating or amusing you, depending on whether you could stand up to him." (Skidmore Owings & Merrill)

Above: This 1964 model shows an Avenue rebuilt from scratch, with National Square intact and most of the Old Post Office swept away. Would people swarm over such a place? Nat Owings vowed they would, even if he had to vend balloons himself. (The President's Council on Pennsylvania Avenue)

Charles Horsky and others recall that the Green Book report was quickly rewritten in simpler language more likely to appeal to Lyndon Johnson. A long historical section by writer Bill Alex was cut to a couple of pages. "The idea kept alive, but just, during the Johnson Administration," Moynihan said. "The counsel to the President, Harry McPherson, was sympathetic, but there was just so much that could be done when it was so much the Kennedys', and with Bobby still on the scene."

Robert J. Lewis, in the *Star*, likened the Kennedy council's Green Book to a topless bathing suit, then a radical fad. Will this plan become a blueprint for change, Lewis asked, "or is it fated only to gather dust as a seven-day wonder that will be of importance only to future bibliographers and antiquarians?" The Green Book was "a beautiful publication worthy of the project," Paul Thiry later

A sketch of a new Market Square, which, like the plan to convert the District Building into an opera house, never materialized. (The President's Council on Pennsylvania Avenue)

recalled. "Whether you agreed with the detail wasn't important. It gave the project, cleaning up Pennsylvania Avenue, importance. But there wasn't anyone in government in a position to provide the momentum. It got in the hands of business people, hoteliers, shoe-store owners, who would be affected, and they recommended changes and lobbied the Hill to accommodate their personal interests." Powerful, critical rumblings began sounding in the press and among other architects. Washington architect Louis Justement excoriated the council's plan as creating another, privatized Federal Triangle on the Avenue's north side. "The private office buildings would be just as deadly at night," the architect wrote in the *Washington Building Congress Bulletin*. It was clear that, to survive, the Pennsylvania Avenue Plan needed powerful help fast.

Its patron dead, the Kennedy council disbanded. It "has dropped this misshapen baby on the Capital's doorstep," as a *Sunday Star* editorial put it, "and promptly folded up." Another commission was set up under Johnson, this one by official executive order. It was called, ominously, the *Temporary* Commission on Pennsylvania Avenue. Owings again chaired it, and many of the same architects continued to contribute. The new commission had a small staff, first headed by John Woodbridge and eventually including design director David Childs, who was brought aboard specifically to develop a housing plan for Market Square. Horsky, who kept his role as D.C.-affairs adviser under the new president, remembered: "Johnson followed through. But it ran into deep trouble [getting funding] on the Hill. I remember standing at President Johnson's elbow one time when a principal congressman came through. He elbowed him, 'Let's get this Pennsylvania Avenue bill out.' 'Yes, Mr. President.' But it never got out."

An adamant opponent, Representative John Saylor of (ironically) Pennsylvania, repelled any and every foray by the Temporary Commission. Once he scolded GSA General Counsel Hart T. Mankin, who had just testified on behalf of a Pennsylvania Avenue bill, for "not knowing much about the history of Washington." "Our founding fathers weren't here in Washington, of course," he began, as if Mankin were an incorrigible child.

They were in Philadelphia. At the time Washington was chosen as the site of the capital the area which you describe as being the vision and dreams of the founding fathers was a swamp. When the founding fathers came to Washington and decided to build the Capitol Hill they faced the Capitol east, and Washington was supposed to grow not in the area you have described, it was supposed to grow toward the Anacostia River.

So please don't ever again make the statement that this [Avenue plan] is going to be the consummation of the dreams and visions of our founding fathers. The founding fathers never conceived of anything down in this swamp.

By 1966, a *Post* headline would read, "The Grand Avenue's National Square Has Been Shunted Away Into Limbo." So had the whole plan.

Childs and others soon realized that the task ahead was not designing, it was lobbying. "Here I was, an architect, out of my league, spending half my time with Pat, going around talking to various people on the Hill." They caught a break following the 1968 elections, when President Nixon brought Moynihan back to town as urban-affairs adviser, working with another special assistant, Peter Flanigan. "Every morning," Childs said,

Pat would go down and take Pennsylvania Avenue issues, which were on Flanigan's desk on the bottom, and put them on top.

[John] Ehrlichman cared about it. He, like other men and women in such a position, found the Pennsylvania Avenue project a relief from daily problems. We would call up, ask for Mr. Ehrlichman's secretary; he would obviously overhear who it was, pick up the phone himself, eager to talk to us. None of us ever knew about the problems that diverted him later with the Watergate mess.

Childs, Owings, and their Temporary Commission produced a report as well, in 1968, now called the Blue Book. It incorporated the design of new GSA buildings (Labor, FBI) and reduced the size of National Square, though still suggesting the destruction of the Washington and Willard hotels. "In many ways history will show that what was originally proposed [in it] and what was later built are exactly the same," Childs, who eventually became a New York partner of Skidmore Owings & Merrill, maintained. "The whole idea of not having government structures on the north side of the Avenue, setbacks, trees, major open spaces on the Avenue. Interestingly enough, the Western Plaza [PADC later] came up with has more hard surfaces than National Square was proposed to have, just a different configuration."

National Square was one of two architectural lightning rods on the Avenue. Mention the other, J. Edgar Hoover's FBI Building, and you're likely to get a snort or guffaw in return. Charles Horsky's characterization of the edifice as "a monstrosity" has been liberally applied to both projects.

General Services Administration counsel Mankin testified before a House subcommittee on national parks in 1970 that the new FBI Building would "be a distinguished structure and will represent the finest in contemporary American architectural thought." But the completed colossus drew nothing but scorn. "Pennsylvania Avenue's a helluva place to have a national police building," Horsky said. But the elephantine structure got past both the Fine Arts and National Capital Planning commissions in 1964 before any of the various Pennsylvania Avenue redevelopment committees could get their hands on it.

According to the FBI's own history, the building is a giant "*box-like* structure" whose original, airy plans were severely modified "to facilitate security." The poured-concrete monolith is surrounded on three sides by what some have called a moat. A forbidding cantilever seems to blot out the moon. "It was constructed to satisfy J. Edgar on the number of square feet he needed to compete with the Justice Department," Horsky remembered. Prolonged appeals from Nat Owings did convince the director to allow a fifty-foot setback from the Avenue, but the FBI controls even the color of brick and the placement of trees in the sidewalk. The PADC spent years convincing the bureau to allow a newsstand kiosk in front of the building.

"Nat wanted to have a passageway on the street level beneath the first floor so you could walk in the rain," said Horsky. "J. Edgar said that would be an invitation to crime." Others wanted to humanize the ground floor with small retail spaces. Hoover and his successors would have none of it. Remembers lawyer and preservationist Bob Peck: "They can't argue security. Any KGB agent who wants to can simply get on the public FBI tour and stick a listening device under somebody's desk. Their next objection was that people who would occupy the retail space behind those concrete, bunker-like panels could somehow tap into the utility system and listen in on conversations. It was crazy stuff." Ben Gilbert and John Fondersmith from the city planning office tried to get Hoover to consider sympathetic ground-floor activities, like an FBI souvenir shop or G-man museum. "No way," remembered Gilbert. "The old man wanted a fortress." Not to worry, the *Post*'s Wolf Von Eckardt wrote in 1979: "The bars and adult bookstores and peep shows that surround the J. Edgar Hoover Building now are presumably so sleazy that no self-respecting foreign agent would go near them." *Washington Star* architectural writer Peter Blake summed up the final product as "a monument to Big Brother." Hulking, overshadowing all that it surveyed, it was also a monument to Big Ego.

Finally, PADC convinced FBI Director William Webster to allow historical panels in front of the concrete facade. "We picked eight Presidents, a variety of them to be featured in silhouette with famous quotes and a collage or pictures from the era," said Executive Director Jay Brodie. "We went up there to try to get them to take down those ugly slabs where stores were supposed to go, and at least make them windows, borrowing exhibits from the Smithsonian, like a traveling museum," said former PADC Chairman Max Berry.

Roger Kennedy [of the Smithsonian] and I go up there, and right away these FBI guys are surrounding me, ganging up on me. They said, "You know, we don't want to turn the Avenue into a circus." I didn't care for that remark, so I said, "Well look, guys, the kiosks and the traveling museum windows are one thing, but when I get through with this, I am coming back, 'cause I got an offer for a merry-go-round, and I am going to put it right out there." These guys are looking at each other like I'm serious. I never told them I was kidding. Interestingly when we got in to see Judge Webster, he was pleasant and cooperative, agreed right away [to the display-window idea, which was later switched to murals].

The FBI Building opened in 1974. At a cost of $126 million ($106 million over 1939 projections for such a structure), it was the most expensive project ever undertaken by the Public Buildings Service. In *Washington Itself*, E. J. Applewhite wrote that the building "did a lot to bring this town together. People from all walks of life who could agree on little else united in cordial dislike of the great hulk." Noted PADC's Brodie, "Thank God the trees out front have grown." Ironically, according to Libby Rowe, chair of the National Capital Planning Commission in the 1960s, except for assurances of adequate security, "Hoover didn't care about the building's design." Rowe added that Hoover had stuck a footnote in her husband's FBI report, which the Rowes had managed to secure, that said, "that's the goddamnedest ugliest building I've ever seen. I don't know why *anybody* would want it."

Unlike Hoover's Nightmare on Pennsylvania Avenue, Nat Owings's National Square was never realized. "Every ceremonial axis needs open terminal areas large enough to produce a sense of celebration and to create a popular gathering place," the President's Council on the Avenue reported in 1964. The council envisioned "the first truly urban, truly national square in the United States." As conceived, the square, just slightly smaller than the Place de la Concorde in Paris, would have ended at a grand gateway to the White House grounds. Wiping out the Willard and Wash-

ington hotels, the National Press Club, and several office buildings, it would have stretched north to F Street, where a "belvedere" — a terrace of outdoor restaurants, planters, and balconies — would have overlooked the Avenue. A freeway, the E Street Expressway, passing underneath the White House grounds and connecting with the Center Leg freeway near the Capitol, would have deposited cars into massive parking garages along E Street. In a paean to his square in the *Christian Science Monitor*, Owings foresaw a "multicolored mass of humanity," a "great outdoor reception room" on the Avenue's west end. "The square was a pleasing design on paper," remembered Rowe. "But looking at squiggles on paper, you don't realize the extent of it. I kept saying, 'We've got plenty of open space in that awful parking lot next to the District Building.'"

At first National Square sailed past regulatory muster. "I was the only person [on her own planning commission] voting against it," Rowe said. "I was painted as an old lady in a hoop-skirt, standing in the way of progress." But the square was soon ridiculed as "the largest frying pan in America." Having already feasted on the "imperial presidency" notion of Richard Nixon to dress White House guards in Prussian helmets, newspapers, who would lose their cozy Press Club, lampooned National Square as "Nixon's Red Square." "Someone at the *Washington Post* asked me why we wanted to tear down the Press Club," said Pat Moynihan, Owings's vice chairman. "I said, 'because it's there.'" *Star* columnist Don McLean began a fanciful campaign to tear down the Treasury Building instead, thus restoring the Avenue's White House view. McLean reported that one supporter wrote, "Your column against the tearing down of the National Press Club and the Occidental Restaurant was the greatest thing I have ever read in my entire life." His admirer, he added, was the owner of the Occidental.

Ohio Senator Frank J. Lausche denounced National Square for "tearing down perfectly good buildings." The world was laughing at Washington, he added. "We are suffering from a mental aberration and delusions of grandeur." Someone suggested that Owings had been spending too much time in the cooling spray of Big Sur and ought to stand for just five minutes in the middle of Pennsylvania Avenue in July to get a true idea of what he was proposing. Fanciful characterizations then and since evoke Rudolph Valentino, crawling hand-over-hand across National Square, pleading, "Water, water."

Above: The plan of the President's Council on Pennsylvania Avenue, a rump committee if there ever was one. Note the dense, swirling patterns of National Square replacing the Willard Hotel. President Nixon took the rap for Nat Owings's idea; people called it "Nixon's Red Square." (The President's Council on Pennsylvania Avenue)

Left: The FBI fortress resisted humanistic efforts to shape it. The superblock of concrete displaced more than one hundred businesses, sealing the Avenue's lifeless gloom for a time. When finished in the early 1970s, J. Edgar Hoover himself called it "The goddamnedest ugliest building I've ever seen. I don't know why anybody would want it." It cost $126 million. (PADC)

Above: The Plaza plan with pylons, mocked in the press as "marble-sized leftovers from the set of *2001*." (Venturi, Rauch and Scott Brown)

Opposite: Architect Robert Venturi's models got a public test in 1981 when this mock-up of the Capitol was erected. Although "the public loved it," the proposal was ridiculed by critics, and the model came tumbling down. (Venturi, Rauch and Scott Brown)

By the time the Pennsylvania Avenue Development Corporation had issued its first plan in 1974, pragmatist Owings had backed off from his dream of one cyclopean square. In its place was a humbler Western Plaza, still huge, still left barren to accommodate public celebrations, but leaving the Willard and Washington intact. Eventually that configuration, too, would be scaled down into two parks, a "hard space" (Western Plaza) and a quiet "green space" (Pershing Park).

The PADC board chose Philadelphia architect Robert Venturi to design Western Plaza. It was a relationship that Venturi would later describe as "a long and sad story." His design incorporated a rectangular grid plan of Washington, in effect a miniature downtown pattern in pavement. The horizontal grid was what Venturi later called "the minor element." The "giant order" was its vertical element, which the PADC agreed was needed to break the barren, flat space: two eighty-six-foot marble pylons, each containing incised quotations from the Constitution and the introduction to the Bill of Rights, framing the view of the Treasury. "School children will use [the pylons] for lessons in government, and perhaps Western Plaza should be called 'We the People Plaza,'" Venturi's firm wrote. In it, the presentation continued, "You can sit on a bench under a shade tree and survey Pulaski, a pool of water, or a tulip bowl. You can lean against a pylon and survey L'Enfant's plan."

Two other "vertical elements" on the plaza were to be models of the White House and Capitol buildings, set on the street grid. For one week, Venturi's firm placed a wooden mock-up of the Capitol on the plaza. "The public loved it," Venturi recalled years later. "It was constantly covered with children and parents, photographing each other."

Ultimately the PADC board backed away from both vertical parts of the Western Plaza proposal. "The pylons seemed to stand for something, some sort of symbol of federal power that the city did not like [in front of its District Building]," Venturi said. "The newly elected mayor [Marion Barry, Jr.] came to a meeting, the first time a mayor had ever gone to a PADC meeting, to go all-out to defeat it." Critics were armed with more newspaper clippings, like the *Star*'s characterization of the pylons as "marble-sized leftovers from the set of *2001*." The pylons as well as the model landmarks, which were mocked as "toys," were both removed from the plan, leaving a flat, open square that, viewed from above, today looks something like the runway pattern at Dulles Airport. "The whole episode was one of the biggest disappointments of my life," recalled Venturi. "It's left terrible memories. The plan was left incomplete — half a plan — and therefore what's left makes not much sense. We realized, too late, that the way things are done in Washington is that you need to hire a lobbyist to lobby your own client [PADC]."

Another vertical concept for the space, what former PADC Executive Director Tom Regan called "Richard Serra's 30-foot-tall series of metal pieces shaped something like a smokestack," was similarly rejected. The only "vertical relief" that the PADC design committee ever approved was the placement of two flagpoles.

Western (now Freedom) Plaza remained a PADC millstone. The staff tried placing potted trees there — in the corners, to preserve the vista — but the effect earned a thumbs-down. Skateboarders slammed into the plaza's edges, damaging them, before being outlawed. "We put chairs there," said PADC Chairman Hank Berliner. "We came down one morning and found that somebody had taken all of the chairs and made a train out of them. There's a whole cadre of people who spend the hours between one and six in the morning doing nothing more than wondering what to do with our chairs." A low-scale fountain for the sizzling space was a later idea under consideration.

M. Paul Friedberg's Pershing Park, a soft, green, urban "bosque," fared far better in both PADC and public esteem, although James M. Goode,

author of *Capital Losses*, called it a "disaster, junked up with too much stuff," replacing an "absolutely beautiful open lawn, well manicured by the Park Service." PADC received many comments, however, that the park had become a pleasant "oasis," where people actually lose themselves in their thoughts, right next to one of the busiest intersections in Washington.

Congress continued to sit on the Temporary Commission's enabling legislation. "Alan Bible was a great help on the Senate side, but Saylor was still obstinate in the House. He would vote no, table it, put it back in committee," said David Childs. "He just didn't want it, period. It was similar to [Joe] Cannon's opposition to the McMillan Plan." Ever-buzzing was Nat Owings. "He would go around and buttonhole people. Like the Ancient Mariner, he'd get the glint in his eye, and you'd know he was going to talk to you about Pennsylvania Avenue." But Saylor's opposition proved telling, and authorization for the Temporary Commission ran out. "I got a call from Pat Moynihan," Childs said. "He asked, 'How's it feel to be fired?'" The six-person staff hung around without portfolio — Childs sequestered at GSA, others elsewhere. But years of work seemed to have gone for naught, downtown Washington festered in despair that followed the 1968 civil disturbances, and the picture of a reborn Pennsylvania Avenue began to flicker and fade.

Above: When Nixon was inaugurated in 1973, the Avenue had reached its nadir. However, the "imperial President" may have really been the one to get revitalization rolling. (Richard M. Nixon Library)

Right: President Nixon's interest helped launch PADC. In 1972 he personally lobbied Congress: "Every month that passes further dims our chances of giving all Americans one birthday present they ought to have — a Capital 'main street' to be proud of." Note Owings to the left: "Nat wrote continually of the Avenue's joie de vivre, which he mispronounced." (PADC)

Life and Transfiguration

ike Hydra, Pennsylvania Avenue redevelopment proved a tough creature to slay. No sooner had the Temporary Commission been dispatched than optimistic new schemes sprang forth to revive the cause. One promising strategy was to wrap the Avenue in the flag, tying it to enthusiasm that was beginning to build for the nation's bicentennial. On September 8, 1970, President Nixon and his urban-affairs adviser, the well-placed Pat Moynihan, took a walking tour of the Avenue. Nixon and Moynihan chatted before scribes and photographers in front of the new, privately financed Presidential Building and gazed at the Capitol Reflecting Pool. That day, the president released a long message in support of House and Senate bills that would establish a Federal City Bicentennial Development Corporation, the first swat at getting a public-private partnership at work on the Avenue. The bills went nowhere, and in 1972 Nixon was back, telling Congress with Owingsesque fervor, "Every month that passes further dims our chances of giving all Americans one birthday present they ought to have—a Capital 'main street' to be proud of."

Congress was skeptical, remembered General Quesada. "They saw it as an end run to sneak in the old Pennsylvania Avenue Plan, which they vehemently opposed. They still visualized those old commissions' models with immense buildings on the north side and that huge National Square." Those "old" commissions had failed to produce a plan that worked for "one simple reason," General Quesada said. "The chairman [Nat Owings] was an architect, and being an architect, he naturally built everything very grandiose. Architects build monuments to themselves." This scowling characterization of architects recalled a viewpoint first raised by Ben McKelway in the *Star* back in the Federal Triangle development days of 1927. "When one architect designs a government building with a mansard roof, another architect is heard loudly sniffling in disgust," McKelway wrote, "recalling that Mansard designed his roof to meet a condition brought about by a French zoning regulation, and that mansard roofs now on government buildings are as useless and out of date as mustache cups at breakfast."

Anyone who "had any sense," General Quesada picked up, "would quickly realize that [previous plans for the Avenue] had no chance of getting the endorsement of Congress. It was blindly irritated by these commissions; they'd become real enemies." By happenstance, Quesada and Owings ended up at the same dinner party at the home of Quesada's good friend, Justin Dart, chairman of Kraft Foods, in Cypress Point, California. "Justin brought Nat Owings's attention to L'Enfant Plaza [the Washington hotel/retail complex that Quesada had also developed]. The conversation then went to Pennsylvania Avenue commissions, and Nat inquired as to why I felt they had not succeeded. I had no hesitancy in telling him."

On Owings's next trip to Washington, the architect told David Childs that he thought he had found, in General Quesada, the ramrod to get a permanent commission past Congress. "I've got just the man,"

Two PADC chairs who made the Avenue move: Elwood "Pete" Quesada, the "bomber of Dresden" who later became a developer, and Hank Berliner. (Yong-Duk Chyun)

Childs remembered Owings saying. "'He's a Republican, a doer, tied to the Republicans on the Hill. I think we can use this guy to get something done.' What he wanted to do was to have Pete Quesada come in, and under Nat's magnificent waving of his hands, get things done. He didn't reckon that Quesada was going to be out there, marshaling the troops. And the general thought Nat would be his sidekick—a miscalculation of the first degree. They started battling immediately."

Little wonder. "I knew the general well as a commander in Belgium," remembered Bill Walton. "He blustered, but sweetness and light don't get you anywhere in Washington." One of Quesada's later executive directors at PADC, W. Anderson "Andy" Barnes, said the general was a "venal individual, enormously temperamental, very interested in his own place in history. He was feared by many, loathed by many, and left a heavy wake of contentiousness." (Barnes did not make the general's Christmas list, either.) According to Ernest A. Connally, "Quesada had no feel at all for urban design. He was a businessman and a planner, the Bomber of Dresden, after all." In 1988 at age eighty-four, Quesada, the man who, as Federal Aviation Agency director, talked Ike into building Dulles International Airport, himself looked back and admitted, "I was mean as hell."

Owings was right about one thing: Quesada was a doer. He became a one-man charge up Capitol Hill on behalf of Pennsylvania Avenue—painting a new, brass-tacks picture of private enterprise locked in loving embrace with the public sector. This turned out to be the "hot button" that finally unlocked the congressional exchequer. After Byzantine negotiations, Congress approved a law establishing a new Pennsylvania Avenue Development Corporation. President Nixon signed the PADC bill on October 27, 1972. Although it as yet had little money, and even less power, there was finally an entity on the scene that had been blessed at both ends of the Avenue.

According to David Childs, a close race ensued between Owings and Quesada to chair this new body. Nixon picked Quesada and appointed an eight-person board of directors. "Nat was philosophical about it," recalled Childs. "He had been there for so long; he said it was just as well to have someone else. It needed someone like Pete Quesada, someone who was 'Damn the torpedoes, full speed ahead.'" John Woodbridge, who had worked with Owings on the old Kennedy council, returned to Washington as PADC's first executive director. He hired a small staff, and yet another round of planning that would result in the third comprehensive plan for Pennsylvania Avenue — PADC's 1974 plan — got underway.

The new commission's general counsel was Peter T. Meszoly, who had worked at GSA and had helped brief Quesada for his assaults on Capitol Hill. "His candor, which at times was excessive at congressional hearings, was one of the main ingredients in getting PADC through Congress," said Meszoly. "I mean, he would go before a committee and say, 'I have no idea how much this or that will cost.' And they loved it." Knowing Quesada's penchant for simplicity, Meszoly said he would lay intricate land transfers, legal briefings, and engineers' reports before the PADC board but give the general a short-and-simple summary. "It got tricky sometimes when he'd ram through these complex deals," Meszoly said. "He ran a very tight meeting. He'd just about mandate each vote. Mrs. [Jouett] Shouse resigned because she said the general was either rude or railroading through the business of the board in about 35 minutes."

True to his congressional testimony, Quesada was a minimalist when it came to the "heavy hand of government" on the private sector. "Sometimes it made it hard to get things done," said Meszoly, "because he was reluctant to exercise the governmental authority the corporation really had." Recalled Quesada, "I had a habit of going before Congress and asking for less than was being offered to me. They weren't used to that. I insisted on keeping the staff size to a minimum; I think that was healthy. It kept us from going the way of all flesh, taking more and more and more." Meszoly said he kept slipping General Quesada notes to "please avoid terms like 'constructive taking' and 'inverse condemnation.' Expressions of genuine sympathy that we have for the owners of distressed properties, OK." Meanwhile Nat Owings, according to Quesada, "wanted to employ a huge staff of architects. I said we had no ability to manage them."

"The early design work involved agonizing reappraisal of the [Kennedy and Johnson commission] plans, including some real fights with Owings, who at first wouldn't even hear of saving the Willard Hotel," recalled Woodbridge. Said John Fondersmith, a District of Columbia planner: "Nat by that time was hot on pueblo ruins — Pueblo Bonito, an Indian ruin in New Mexico. He'd got interested in low buildings and was 'anti-skyscraper' — this, from a guy who made his money and reputation building high-rises. I think that translated into his interest in a Hill Town." The Italian Hill Town was a plan, never realized, to develop a massive, bowl-shaped residential and office complex at Market Square.

Executive Director Woodbridge was described by those who knew him as an intellectual idealist, a superb designer who articulately pitched his PADC architectural plans. Meszoly and others recall Woodbridge gathering the staff for lofty discussions on the meaning of good art and architecture. Staff architects came back from trips to Europe with slide shows of the best ideas in urban design. Job definitions were so loose in PADC's formative years that Meszoly issued a directive to keep him informed of any contacts with Congress, lest some clerk make a policy decision. "Obviously, I do not mean to limit your rights to petition the Congress for redress of grievances, as guaranteed by the Constitution," Meszoly told them, tongue firmly in cheek. "So this memorandum applies only to PADC matters and not personal matters you wish to transact with the Congress. Yours in the law, . . ."

All this bonhomie irritated the impatient General Quesada. "We'd had enough planning," he said. "It was time to start doing." Problem was, the PADC was limping along on skimpy (by federal standards) appropriations — "maybe a million dollars a year," according to Quesada. "We weren't allowed to acquire any land, and we were subjected to all sorts of influence by special interests, who wanted to restrict the land for their own self-interests. John Woodbridge, to his credit, resisted all that in a mighty way. He kept his idea straight ahead."

Progress was slow in prying loose dollars with which to get the "D" (for Development) in PADC going. "After two weeks of ceaseless prodding, the bastards at the Treasury Department are finally prepared to cough up our draft legislation," Meszoly complained in a note to the Office of Management and Budget. "They took over four weeks reviewing a three-page draft bill on which expeditious action was repeatedly requested. May their bank vaults crumble!"

Legislation fully arming PADC with sufficient budget plus Treasury borrowing power to purchase property — and the dreaded power of eminent domain should landholders be uncooperative — became entangled. Then one day in March 1976 the full House caught PADC flatfooted: It defeated the PADC funding bill for fiscal 1977 and adjourned before Quesada and his squadron could react. "We were encouraged to begin looking for other jobs," recalled Yong-Duk Chyun, then a PADC staff architect. "Fortunately, I didn't find one." Chyun later became the corporation's design and planning director and one of its graybeards.

Above: In 1980, stonemason Joe Musolino directed his crew as they prepared to place one of hundreds of carefully etched stones on new Western Plaza. The park was nearly complete, but much controversy remained over Robert Venturi's planned additions of models of the Capitol and White House and two huge pylons. (Washingtoniana Division, D.C. Public Library)

Opposite top: Street vendors helped liven things while the Avenue was a work-in-progress. (Carol M. Highsmith)

Opposite bottom: What would the Victor of Gettysburg have thought of the assorted wood nymphs surrounding him in Charles A. Grafly's 1927 Meade Monument? He would probably rather be keeping company with the history buffs who came to celebrate Meade's restoration to the Avenue after fifteen years in storage. (Carol M. Highsmith)

Stunned that its well-laid plans for "doing" had again been undermined on the Hill, the PADC board and staff set to work on a classic big-league, Washington-style lobbying effort. They "manipulated press coverage," according to Meszoly. "We got the Federal City Council, which was very tight with the *Washington Post*, behind us," he said. The staff "schmoozed," to use his word, friends in the House like Roy A. Taylor of North Carolina, who chaired the key subcommittee on national parks. Meszoly drafted two "dear colleague" letters to be signed by supportive House members, one to go to those who voted against the PADC bill, the other to those who did not vote. And Meszoly even organized a "moot hearing," with himself, Woodbridge, and David Harris playing themselves and junior staffers role-playing subcommittee members throwing hardball questions.

Schmoozing paid off. In August 1976, Congress reversed itself, authorizing two-year funding of PADC and requiring preservation of the Willard Hotel. Thus began the PADC strategy to develop a "success story" on the west end of the Avenue before moving to improve the east. The FBI Building and its moat would be the dividing line. On August 14, 1976, more than fifteen years after John F. Kennedy and Arthur Goldberg had first resolved to "fix" Pennsylvania Avenue, President Gerald R. Ford signed the first bill to give any entity significant funds to the get the fixing done. The bill authorized spending $38 million on parks, greenery, streetlighting, and repaving.

Woodbridge's comprehensive Pennsylvania Avenue Plan of 1974 — the third try at a blueprint for the Avenue — downsized the mighty west-end square, kept the Willard and Press Club, and proposed the residential Italian Hill Town. It took advantage of a sort of loophole in Washington's famous 130-foot height limitation. Recalled Woodbridge, "In the 1910 buildings act, they'd provided for an exception for the north side of Pennsylvania Avenue, allowing a height of 160 feet. We were able to use it as leverage with developers: 'You can go higher, but you have to give us a greater setback.'" The taller buildings would help frame the Avenue's sight lines, and the setbacks would restore room for trees, benches, and promenading.

In 1977, Woodbridge left the commission to open a private practice near San Francisco. He was succeeded, in turn, by three other men of vastly different backgrounds, each proving to be a good match for his time. Design Director Chyun assessed them:

Andy Barnes, a former real-estate broker and White House fellow and, according to Meszoly, "young comer." Said Chyun, "In spite of the publicity about him [Barnes drew a flurry of bad press for arranging to get a large cash bonus, over General Quesada's opposition], he brought a strong business background that helped kick off development competition. We went from a great planner and architect to someone who knew how to put a business plan together." Said Barnes:

What really put us over the top in getting something done was to follow the advice of some of my bureaucratic friends, who told me to apply for a budget slightly more than we'd really like to receive. What we decided to do instead was to *double* our budget request. We did so with the expectation that Washington in its charming way would ultimately cut it approximately in half. Instead we got it all, and we had to scramble to figure how to responsibly spend it. It turned out we used every penny of it, because it enabled us to move faster in acquiring parcels, to go to the business community and say, "Listen, guys, Congress is really serious about us."

Tom Regan, an engineer promoted from within when Barnes left in 1982 for the West Coast — Valhalla for former Pennsylvania Avenue planners. Chyun's evaluation: "Tom really got the public improvements done, the parks, the plazas, the roads, and the sidewalks. He was an excellent construction-management type with a down-to-earth style. No contractors ever tried to fool him. He set clear schedules and kept to them." It was on Regan's watch that Pershing Park and Western Plaza took shape where traffic islands and a betuliped city common had once clumped.

Finally, in 1984, when Regan left to join a development firm, along came *M. J. "Jay" Brodie*, an architect who had been commissioner of Baltimore's Department of Housing and Community Development. "He came with the mission to get housing going. The housing plan had been adjusted to be more realistic, and Jay helped keep it afloat when it looked like it was not going anywhere. Because of him, the momentum for housing on the Avenue continued."

PADC began to tick off one coup after another. According to one of General Quesada's successors as chairman, Henry A. Berliner, Jr., PADC will have realized, by the time "sunset" — the expiration of its enabling legislation — hits in 1992: more than a dozen mixed-use projects up and down the Avenue, attracting $1.3 billion in private sector development money; $100 million spent on public improvements, including six new parks, better lighting, roadbed and sidewalks, and seven hundred new willow oak trees; a gigantic new Canadian Chancery; an arts district; and at least the stirrings of housing.

One of the north-side buildings to be rehabilitated under PADC auspices was the Pennsylvania Building, overlooking Western Plaza. It had been the last private office building constructed before the area's precipitous decline. "The expression, 'being where the action is,' certainly applies to us and this building," said Richard S. Cohen, president of Willco Construction Co., Inc., which refurbished the Pennsylvania.

Look at those great turn-of-the-century photographs, and you'll see people passing ten or twelve abreast outside the little Hotel Johnson on this site, although it was just as likely that it was the Pennsylvania Railroad ticket office or Warwick's Billiard Parlor drawing the crowd. Of course less-exuberant days of the north side of the Avenue saw a nondescript office building here, and a parking lot and a gas station down the block. I think it was the Secretary of the Interior's survey in 1974 that described the old Pennsylvania Building as "a poor expression of the ribbon fenestration pattern popular for commercial buildings of its period." Let's just say it was an unremarkable frame for the important west end of this great Avenue. When we bought the Pennsylvania Building in 1966, it did not even have a Pennsylvania Avenue address. It was "425 Thirteenth Street, Northwest." They actually thought a Thirteenth Street address was more prestigious. That's how little was the stature of Pennsylvania Avenue. By the time we got involved in renovating and reopening the building [in 1985], the fireworks had died down over what to put in Western Plaza, and how big to make it. We could finally look out and see the promise of plans laid to paper coming to life. And we definitely wanted that Pennsylvania Avenue address.

So facile was PADC in stimulating development that the General Services Administration and the Federal City Council pushed through — on a rare unanimous vote in Congress under the ubiquitous Moynihan's skillful whip — approval of a new, 3.1-million-square-foot International Cultural and Trade Center. They asked PADC to take the lead role in designing and developing it, even though the land was outside its jurisdiction. The ICTC filled what Moynihan called the "missing tooth in the otherwise-beautiful smile of Pennsylvania Avenue" — the Great Plaza parking lot next to the District Building. The ICTC, second-largest federal building in the nation, behind the Pentagon, was created to consolidate State and Justice department functions; provide space for international exhibits and trade shows; and dangle, along with the Old Post Office Pavilion, a lure for the millions of tourists on the Mall. Council President Harry McPherson called the ICTC "a winner on the Avenue."

Above: Richard S. Cohen, president of Willco Construction Company, which refurbished the Pennsylvania Building. (Carol M. Highsmith)

Left: The designers of the Pennsylvania Building renovation, Robert J. McMahon (left), vice president, and Robert Calhoun Smith, president, Smith-McMahon Architects, P.C. (Carol M. Highsmith)

Opposite: In 1987 the Pennsylvania Building was remodeled, re-covered with Alabama limestone, and given an Avenue address. In 1966 it had been sited to face Thirteenth Street. (Carol M. Highsmith)

138

An almost unanimously praised PADC triumph, too, was its stunning series of public improvements, which turned Pennsylvania Avenue into a linear city park. Its dozens of flower-stuffed urns, surprising green spaces, and hundreds of trees change texture with the seasons. New pedestrian lighting that shines upward, into the leaves, as well as splaying the decorative sidewalks, softens the scene at night. Even the forbidding buildings of the Federal Triangle have an added moon glow. There's an unconscious list to the Avenue as foot traffic hugs the south side in winter, because the warming sun is there, and steers for north-side shade come the sweltering Washington summer.

Each spring and summer, decorative grasses and flowering lantana start so tentatively that they've been mistaken for weeds and pulled by passersby trying to be helpful. Autumn perfectly states a cooling breeze, a break in the torpor, a welcome drying look everywhere, vivid fall colors jumping alive in Pershing Park and John Marshall Park. Crape myrtle, rustling grasses, and black-eyed susans at Pershing suggest a farmer's pond. The Avenue makes an overall statement — its willow oaks just now, with a decade's growth, beginning to suggest a canopy. The oaks hold their leaves well into winter, keeping barrenness at bay.

Spring is a broadcloth bouquet of tulips and daffodils, a sensual stirring. The Avenue of summer is sultry, indolent. Thunderstorms roil. Umbrellas sprout like mushrooms. Russets, fire reds, straw grasses cover the hard edges in fall. But winter is a most memorable time as well, of snow carnivals and sliding cars, cold moons over the deep-purple sky above the Capitol dome, bells and twinkling Christmas lights and juniper berries.

The Pennsylvania Avenue of the mid-1970s was dominated by plastic-looking hedges, trimmed at the sidewalk edge to look crisp, neat, properly institutional. Poorly maintained, they presented a remarkably ugly pastiche. What changed things was a realization by PADC Executive Director Tom Regan that something looked brighter and far more pleasing in another public space, the Virginia Avenue Garden at the Martin Building — the Federal Reserve Annex—which Regan passed each day to and from work. Once a dead space above a parking garage, that plaza had turned into a visual delight, enjoyable even in passing at forty miles per hour. A couple of phone calls, and he was meeting with the Virginia Garden's design team, Oehme, van Sweden & Associates. Wolfgang Oehme, a Berlin-educated horticulturist and landscape architect, and James A. van Sweden, Dutch-trained

landscape architect, were hired as planting consultants to PADC, and the change from concrete-drab to a dramatic panache was on.

When they began, said van Sweden, "We saw the usual plants—you could list about eight—junipers, ivy, some trees, hedges. They were planted in clipped rows." Oehme, van Sweden started by replanting in front of Federal Triangle buildings, taking out hollies and boxlike hedges, keeping some of the azaleas — even though, noted van Sweden, "we're famous for hating azaleas." They regrouped the plants, gave several to the National Park Service, and added perennials. Then they redid Pershing Park, injecting dramatic American and Chinese grasses, smoky fountain grasses, and more perennials. Instead of clipping the greenery at the edge of hard spaces, they allowed plants to overhang, casting a moody lavender splash of unpredictability to the unfriendly marble. "Everything was softened. It added a kind of drama that people love," said van Sweden. "It took eight years," he added, but Oehme, van Sweden "finally got a chance to plant the pond" at Pershing Park, dropping in water lilies, lotuses, and other plants.

Opposite: Pershing Park provides an all-season display where plastic-looking hedges once dominated. (Carol M. Highsmith)

Above: Landscape architects James A. van Sweden (left) and Wolfgang Oehme have brought a touch of wilderness to the Avenue. (Carol M. Highsmith)

Oehme, van Sweden also worked on the hottest, hardest space on the Avenue: Western Plaza. They yanked out hedge yews and added sun-loving perennials, such as Russian sage, and more ornamental grasses. They also addressed Robert Venturi's futuristic urns at the plaza. "He said they should be planted to look like Edwardian women's hats," said van Sweden.

He did a drawing of them in which they looked like a bouquet of flowers. The question was, what do you do with them? They're aluminum, and the sun beats down and reflects up from underneath. They got to 140 degrees. What kind of plant will live there, and how are you going to make them look like an Edwardian woman's hat? Wolfgang and I proposed lantana around the outside — it's tough, loves heat — and red geraniums and white begonias, topped up with tropical yucca that looks like a big feather. It gets a bloom on top as well.

After a few weeks, everyone assessed the effect. "Awful!" van Sweden said. "We found out they weren't being watered properly. Someone would stand there [he gestured like a man spraying a water hose in fifty directions] and walk away. We said, 'You have to stand there for *twenty minutes per pot* and don't go away until water pours out the bottom.'" He and his partner also managed to convince PADC to allow plants — cattails, water iris — in the spillover fountain in Western Plaza. "No sooner had we finished than a family of ducks moved in," van Sweden said.

An Oehme, van Sweden staff member, along with representatives of PADC, a local nursery, and the Park Service, walked the Avenue once a week, checking for damage and theft, spotting plants that were failing, and assuring that irrigation was successful. Plantings in more than two hundred pots along the Avenue were changed each season — tulips, planted in fall for blooming in spring, junipers for winter, and the mix of grasses and perennials in the summer and fall. The result of the entire Avenue plan, according to a *Washington Post* review of Oehme, van Sweden's work: "a landscape revolution."

One criticism of PADC centered on the lack of a stunning architectural success on the Avenue. Even its first executive director, Woodbridge, commented, "We had some of the most eminent architects in America produce some of their most mediocre work." Robert L. Miller, in *Historic Preservation* magazine, wrote, "The Avenue seemed a hodge podge of developers' and preservationists' conflicting visions. . . . To an extent unimaginable in most American cities, Pennsylvania Avenue is not merely a camel, the proverbial horse designed by

committee. It's a whole genus of camels, a Galapagos of partially evolved camel prototypes, each of whose fossils remain to be supplanted a few years later by another equally short-lived attempt at a new species." The *Post*'s business magazine called the new J. W. Marriott Hotel, in the heart of PADC's showcase west end, "particularly ugly." In helping dedicate the reopened Willard Hotel, Senator Moynihan extolled that sparkling renovation, then drew gasps by pointing to the Marriott next door. "Anything," he said, "is better than *that*."

Lawyer and preservationist Robert Peck complained of PADC: "Its main plan for restoring buildings is to put facades in storage. It's an architectural Disneyland concept" — a reference to PADC's saving the facades of buildings, some of which were cracking during Metro subway construction, storing them at the National Arboretum, and reassembling them wholesale or in cornice, lintel, and doorway pieces in other projects.

Peck continued: "In many cases PADC had to be dragged, kicking and screaming, into saving some of the historic buildings. They didn't want the Willard or the Old Post Office at first." Peck also faulted the development corporation for not "doing more to animate the Avenue. . . . What about bars, or organ grinders and vendors? Why not do what Rouse did at Faneuil Hall [in Boston] and Harborplace [Baltimore]: pay magicians, acrobats, and jugglers to show up and draw a crowd? They're afraid that it might get tacky." Even former chairman Max N. Berry wondered, "I had a high-school kid go out with a two thousand dollar popcorn machine and sell popcorn on the Avenue. We made money on it the first summer. Whatever happened to that popcorn machine?" Nat Owings once said he'd sell balloons on National Square, if necessary, to draw a crowd.

Executive Director Brodie pointed to an extensive arts project along Seventh Street, up from the Avenue in PADC territory. It included redeveloping the Lansburgh's block as a residence and cultural center, the attraction of art galleries to the street, and underwriting a Washington Project for the Arts location. Noted Chairman Berliner, "if you fail to have the arts, it's like a meal without wine."

PADC's own chief designer, Chyun, said he regretted that there were not more shops and restaurants along the Avenue, and he faulted the organization for not developing a more aggressive retail plan. "We've had many vague notions," he said. "But we've not really done anything other than this wish or that desire. In my opinion we could have struck a deal with developers to make sure

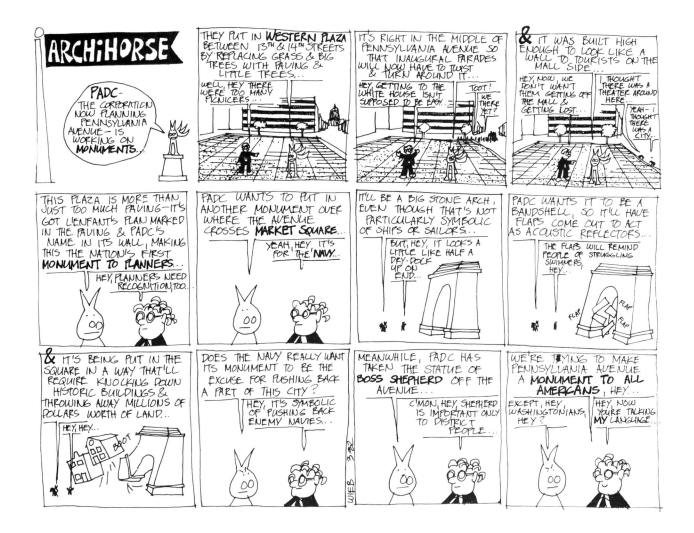

[lively ground-floor retail] happened, realizing that bars and restaurants and other interesting retail establishments cannot pay high rent." Chyun, however, vigorously defended the architectural plan of the Avenue. "For us the most important thing was to define Pennsylvania Avenue as space. We cannot afford freestanding monuments by all these architects. We needed buildings that would be subservient to the Avenue as space in the manner of baroque city design."

Iconoclastic Washington architect John Wiebenson, who, using a cartoon newsletter character named "Archihorse," ridiculed various PADC plans, faulted PADC's lack of progress on getting reasonably priced housing on the Avenue. "The board chairmen wanted to show [ledger] books with no money lost [through subsidizing housing]. Well, how could anyone blame them if they lost money? But housing, in their minds, was too risky." Archihorse's creator knew, as did PADC from experience, that ridicule could kill a Pennsylvania Avenue project, as it did when the U.S. Navy's noodling of a grand arch at its memorial was sniggeringly dismissed as a "McDonald's arch."

In the 1970s, Washington architect John Wiebenson criticized PADC efforts in a sarcastic cartoon series. Such ridicule helped kill several Avenue proposals, including one for a memorial navy arch. Robert Venturi's planned pylons on Western Plaza, for instance, were mocked as "phallic symbols," his scale models of the White House and Capitol called "toys." National Square was lampooned as "Nixon's Red Square." (John Wiebenson, *Progressive Review*)

But former PADC Executive Director Regan stuck up vehemently for PADC and its accomplishments.

It has been consistent, free from taint, strictly straight in dealing in the volatile world of real estate, and that's not easy. PADC's board would negotiate, but there was always a line of principle and adherence to both the letter and spirit of the plan that it would not cross, just for expediency, to make a deal. On balance, PADC is one of the most successful public-private joint ventures ever to exist in this country. I think people will look at it twenty years from now and say, "My God, here's a federal agency that did what it said it was going to do, in a professional, ethical, way, with sympathy and respect for the urban design."

Above: In 1988, Western Plaza was rededicated as Freedom Plaza in memory of Martin Luther King, Jr. Here Coretta Scott King supervises the installation of a time capsule containing items from Dr. King's life. (Carol M. Highsmith)

Right: The redeveloped Avenue "lifts our spirits," said Mac Asbill, Jr., a partner in Sutherland, Asbill & Brennan, Attorneys at Law. "The PADC has indeed created an American Champs-Elysées." (Carol M. Highsmith)

Opposite: Western Plaza celebration of the 1980s: Life is cracking through Mellon's Great Wall of Government. (Carol M. Highsmith)

PADC earned accolades from many professionals and business executives along the Avenue as well. "By its magnificent revitalization of the Avenue, the Pennsylvania Avenue Development Corporation has given the city and the nation a boulevard of which they can be proud," said attorney Mac Asbill, Jr., a partner in Sutherland, Asbill & Brennan.

The Avenue links many elements of our national life and heritage. It physically connects the legislative and executive branches, and many important courts. It brings together government, finance, the professions, retail business of all sorts, entertainment, and many of our treasured museums and cultural monuments. In addition, through a major embassy and the soon-to-be-developed International Cultural and Trade Center, it links us with our partners around the world. It provides a focal point for the celebration of local and national accomplishments, ranging from the Super Bowl victory of our Redskins to the inauguration of our president. By its physical beauty and the inspiring — almost festive —

atmosphere of areas such as Freedom Plaza, it lifts our spirits. In the Avenue, the PADC has indeed created an American Champs-Elysées.

Max Berry, back in the practice of trade law in Georgetown, remembered: "Fiscal conservatives on the Hill looked at us as liberal spendthrifts. They thought that we would be another government agency that would take a bath, so let's let private enterprise take care of Pennsylvania Avenue. Well, look at the results: Private money came in ten-to-one over government money." Ironically, it was liberal Democrat Berry who antagonized some of his own staff by imposing spending limits, requiring that they fly tourist class, cutting out "all these trips to study the squares of Rome," and putting a cap on expense accounts. "I had the Canadians out and bought 'em chili dinners out of my own pocket," he said. "It wasn't that I was such a tight-ass. We had a budget, and we were going to stick to it."

145

Berry's successor as chairman, Hank Berliner, recalled arguments that the western end of the Avenue, closer to the White House and attractions like the National Theatre, would have improved by itself, that PADC would have been wiser to throw money and attention at the less-promising eastern end. "I believe the way you start in a blighted area is to start with your strength, not your weakness," he said.

In the banking business, we don't start making resort loans to build five miles from the ocean and hope someday to work gradually to the beach. We start building on the oceanfront, which is the final attraction, and gradually build back. . . . To say we should have expended half of our resources at this end and half at the other end and hope that sometime they would meet in the middle would have been a disaster. There is a point at which you get an explosion of interest that acquires such a critical mass that it allows the whole to succeed. If we'd tried to do it piecemeal, it wouldn't have been successful.

Berliner said he had met with Undersecretary of the Treasury George Gould. "We have the prospect of having on hand about $55 million when we close up in 1992," he said. "We'd like to repay the Treasury, but because the Treasury has engaged in long-term financing of PADC over 30 years, they have a stream of payments that they are expecting. They don't want us to pay it back!"

So the "planning" of Nat Owings and John Woodbridge and the "doing" of Pete Quesada had finally resulted in a makeover of the "disgrace" that had been Pennsylvania Avenue. "Let's not forget one key group of players all along the way,"

reminded Pat Moynihan. "There were dark days, real discouraging days. But people in the District business community — the Federal City Council, Downtown Progress, the Greater Washington Board of Trade — never stopped pushing. Others got the glory, but these people did a lot of the thankless spadework."

"We all realized that downtown as a whole could not come back if the Avenue were still a national disgrace," said Board of Trade President Delano E. Lewis. As a C&P Telephone, Washington Company president, Lewis had supervised enormous telecommunications projects on the Avenue — everything from the 1987 Reagan-Gorbachev summit to presidential inaugurations every four years — for both C&P and parent company Bell Atlantic.

Just as PADC was doing its good work, attitudes about cities and city life began to change. The suburbs might be comfortable, but people again came to appreciate the ambience, the energy, of what's sometimes called "the urban experience." Pennsylvania Avenue renovations were a showcase, a demonstration project. They helped us tell the real story of downtown's vitality. And they helped people reconnect with downtown as the place to be. Once that happened, all kinds of good things started to fall into place in the District of Columbia.

By his firm's calculation, real estate broker Julien J. Studley was responsible for 70 percent of the moves of tenants to the "new downtown," beginning with the shift of the National League of Cities into what became the American Cities Building at Thirteenth and the Avenue. Another Studley ten-

ant, the law firm of Squire Sanders & Dempsey, led a parade into the new 1201 Pennsylvania Avenue. Another of the city's prominent law firms, Covington & Burling, soon followed into the building's top floors. Julien Studley said: "It took us two years to convince one firm to move to the Avenue. Two years! We researched the hotels, the safety record, the fact that PADC had delivered on every one of its promises about the Avenue. And when people saw the quality of the ownership and the quality of the developers who took a chance on Pennsylvania Avenue, they came on board. Once confidence was restored, people knew what that address and that view could mean for business."

When Perpetual Savings Bank sought a site for its new corporate banking headquarters and financial center, it picked a location on the inaugural route, at the point where Pennsylvania and New York avenues and Fifteenth street all converge. According to Thomas J. Owen, chairman and chief executive officer:

This section of the Avenue corridor has been the financial heart of the city and of the nation, too, in a way, because of all the government activity. A great deal of our financial activity involves real estate matters and transactions with companies based outside the city, and we wanted a strategic location that "suggests" Washington and represents solidity. Here, across from the Treasury where a number of banks and savings and loans got their start, was a prestigious, substantial location. After so many years of decline, Pennsylvania Avenue is again the place to be.

What comes after PADC? Even admirers fear that the Avenue will revert to less-noble, mercenary interests; that the great Pennsylvania Plan of twenty years' and three commissioners' labors will crumble for lack of a champion; that its green spaces, left to functionaries who treat them like somebody's backyard to water, will not be given the loving attention that has built a verdant streetscape; that attention will drift elsewhere. Max Berry championed a Pennsylvania Avenue Foundation, modeled after Rockefeller Center's in New York. Jay Brodie talked about "not retreating to what Kennedy saw in '61, making sure we keep it at least as good as what we have achieved today, finding a way to sustain it the way every city in the world has sustained its great boulevards, by looking after it and, periodically, giving it shots of adrenaline."

Others said they wanted to see a trimmed-down PADC itself kept around to police the L'Enfant vision. "Of course," chuckled Berliner, "Let's all remember that L'Enfant was fired!"

Opposite top: Banks once redlined the Avenue. Now they're doing business on the boulevard as never done before. "The Avenue is again the place to be," said Thomas J. Owen, chairman and CEO of Perpetual Savings Bank. (Carol M. Highsmith)

Opposite bottom: The Avenue's surge coincided with downtown revival in the District of Columbia, contended Delano E. Lewis, president, C&P Telephone, Washington Company. (Carol M. Highsmith)

Above: Julien J. Studley, Inc., formerly had to *lobby* its clients to locate on the Avenue. Pictured are corporate vice presidents Jeff K. Shrago and Lois A. Zambo. (Carol M. Highsmith)

Overleaf: A Pennsylvania Avenue Development Corporation map of its projects. Inset shows the same streets fifty years ago. (PADC)

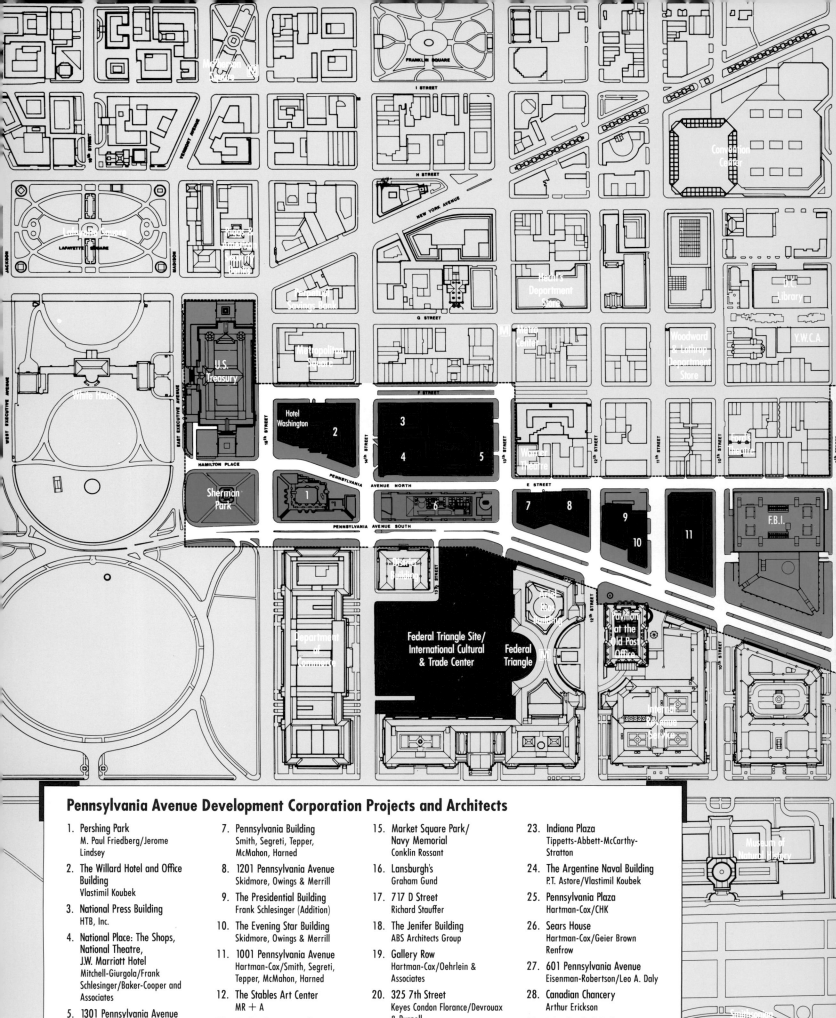

Pennsylvania Avenue Development Corporation Projects and Architects

1. **Pershing Park**
   M. Paul Friedberg/Jerome Lindsey

2. **The Willard Hotel and Office Building**
   Vlastimil Koubek

3. **National Press Building**
   HTB, Inc.

4. **National Place: The Shops, National Theatre, J.W. Marriott Hotel**
   Mitchell-Giurgola/Frank Schlesinger/Baker-Cooper and Associates

5. **1301 Pennsylvania Avenue**
   Frank Schlesinger

6. **Freedom Plaza**
   Venturi, Rauch and Scott Brown/ George Patton

7. **Pennsylvania Building**
   Smith, Segreti, Tepper, McMahon, Harned

8. **1201 Pennsylvania Avenue**
   Skidmore, Owings & Merrill

9. **The Presidential Building**
   Frank Schlesinger (Addition)

10. **The Evening Star Building**
    Skidmore, Owings & Merrill

11. **1001 Pennsylvania Avenue**
    Hartman-Cox/Smith, Segreti, Tepper, McMahon, Harned

12. **The Stables Art Center**
    MR + A

13. **Market Square North**
    Martin & Jones

14. **Market Square**
    Hartman-Cox/Morris

15. **Market Square Park/ Navy Memorial**
    Conklin Rossant

16. **Lansburgh's**
    Graham Gund

17. **717 D Street**
    Richard Stauffer

18. **The Jenifer Building**
    ABS Architects Group

19. **Gallery Row**
    Hartman-Cox/Oehrlein & Associates

20. **325 7th Street**
    Keyes Condon Florance/Devrouax & Purnell

21. **625 Indiana Avenue**
    Brennan Beer Gorman

22. **Bob Hope USO Building**
    Guiliani Associates

23. **Indiana Plaza**
    Tippetts-Abbett-McCarthy-Stratton

24. **The Argentine Naval Building**
    P.T. Astore/Vlastimil Koubek

25. **Pennsylvania Plaza**
    Hartman-Cox/CHK

26. **Sears House**
    Hartman-Cox/Geier Brown Renfrow

27. **601 Pennsylvania Avenue**
    Eisenman-Robertson/Leo A. Daly

28. **Canadian Chancery**
    Arthur Erickson

29. **John Marshall Park**
    Carol R. Johnson

30. **Meade Plaza**
    Bernard Johnson, Inc.

Washington architect Hugh Jacobsen's plan for an Italianate Hill Town on the Avenue, including 850 apartments: "[The PADC board] was looking at me like I was totally insane. Nat stood back in the corner, actually pumping his hand at me as if to say, 'Go, go . . . great!'" The Hill Town concept was called "fascist" and elitist. It went the way of Venturi's pylons. (PADC)

By all accounts, from the moment he sat down to doodle the assignment just given him by Arthur Goldberg at President Kennedy's behest in 1962, Nathaniel Owings was determined that a component of the plan to revitalize Pennsylvania Avenue would be an infusion of housing. "Nat wrote continually of the Avenue's joie de vivre, which he mispronounced," remembered David Childs. "He, solely, wanted housing on the Avenue. No one else on the commission cared about it. He said it would bring life to the Avenue. He even wanted schools, which I thought was a terrible idea. Nat had this sort of Jeffersonian vision of a low-scale development."

Owings and his fellow commissioners were vague about housing at first, referring only to "superblocks" midway down the Avenue that would include "middle-income housing," hotels, and restaurants — a modern re-creation of a nineteenth-century neighborhood, "an old town within the new town." Housing units would bring people to the Avenue twenty-four hours a day, Owings reasoned, creating a Greenwich Village feel to what had become a desolate urban graveyard after dark. "We need the housing," editorialized the *Post*. "We need people to live on the Avenue to keep it lively around the clock and sustain the shops and restaurants that must be sustained, if Pennsylvania Avenue is ever to be anything more than a longitudinal mausoleum where magnificent intentions and federal vainglory are buried." There certainly was a void to fill: A survey done for Congress in the early 1970s would find only thirteen housing units in the entire Pennsylvania Avenue corridor.

It took the new PADC to come up with a concrete housing proposal. "I once said to Nat Owings that every architect wants to do two things," Patrick Moynihan remembered. "One is duplicating Paris. The other is an Italian Hill Town. They had Paris [in L'Enfant's and various commissions' own plans]. So they got Hugh Jacobsen to give them a Hill Town." When Owings approached him on behalf of PADC, Washington architect Hugh Newell Jacobsen had established a firm reputation as a designer of housing in the private sector. "But here was my chance at immortality," he jested in remembering the moment.

Most people carry pictures of their grandchildren in their wallets. Nat carried a picture of housing. We had a snappy dinner at some Mexican place — Nat, David Childs, and I — flamenco dancers, the works. Once we could concentrate, I was awed by Nat and his work.

After several briefings, I came up with this scheme of a megastructure, addressing itself to the monumentality of the Avenue, recalling the days of Market Square. It was a chance to reform that square.

PADC's plan called for 1,500 housing units — 850 of them in the Hill Town. It spilled in a sort of amphitheater back from a white-limestone facade, inset with windows, along the Avenue, sixteen stories high and full of offices and the headquarters of the new Woodrow Wilson Center for Scholars. The facade, part of the planned street-wall effect along the length of the Avenue's north side, would be broken at Eighth Street. The interior contained apartments for the visiting scholars, as well as other housing units that fell in a stepped pattern to create what Jacobsen called "a large bowl."

Jacobsen briefed the PADC board. "I was nervous as a counterfeiter before all those heavyweights," he said. "They were looking at me like I was totally insane. Nat stood back in the corner, actually pumping his hand at me as if to say, 'Go, go . . . great!' " They took their model to the White House to brief the vice president.

I had it in my snappy new Camaro, and when I pulled in, the guard gave me the dirtiest look. Nat and John Woodbridge and I took it upstairs, and Jerry Ford spoke very kindly about it. Nat talked about it — you know, an architect never "sells," he "presents." We talked for about an hour, and I carried the model back out to my car, and another beady-eyed guard looked at me like I was a saboteur. I couldn't figure out why until I got home, and my son took me around back of my car.

"You went there with *that!*" he said. He was pointing at my IMPEACH NIXON bumper sticker.

The Hill Town idea "cleared all the commissions — cleared 'em all," Jacobsen remembered. "But it all slipped away. A lack of momentum killed it. Every project has a heartbeat, a rhythm. If it goes out of synch, it dies. The project just sat there." In fact the Hill Town had become a controversial hot spot. Critics said it was "fascist," that it would attract only the rich, that it was designed (not long after riots had marred the area) to keep out the real life of the city. "It was a walled city," remembered Childs, "or it gave that impression: a white, walled, isolated, high-cost city." "Not so," said Jacobsen. "There were no barricades. Eighth Street was open. The elevators were open."

What in fact killed the Hill Town? Critics said it would be too costly to rip out the huge Potomac Electric Power Company transformer substation at Eighth and D streets. The Wilson scholars, located "temporarily" at the old Smithsonian Castle, loved it there, and never again looked at Pennsylvania Avenue. PADC wrestled with the reality that it would have to write down land values and make up the difference with subsidies. Others argued that housing made no sense in a monumental corridor. Even in 1988, Libby Rowe asked, "Who's going to live down there? Maybe two young people, no children, two fat salaries."

The corporation envisioned a range of prices for rental units and condominiums, one-third available to low-income households. But, according to PADC's first general counsel, Pete Meszoly, that was a sop to Mayor Walter Washington, who had insisted on a mix that included low-income households. "Nobody would say it publicly [at a time of intense pressure for affirmative action], but anybody with any sense realized if you're going to have housing down there at all, it certainly isn't going to be low or even moderate [-priced]. The Hill Town plan died when low-income supporters kept talking about 'housing for the elite.' So what did they get instead: nothing, a major absence of life." Ben Gilbert, Mayor Washington's economic-development director, admitted that "the housing question went through the Perils of Pauline. Yes, we wanted a range of income levels. But it was symbolic, more than anything. We weren't going to turn Pennsylvania Avenue into a housing project." According to the *Washington Post*, "Low-income units were dropped from the [PADC] plan in 1981, the victim of a dramatic rise in land costs, soaring interest rates, and a decision by the Reagan administration to oppose housing subsidies."

Right: The Market Square development team. From left to right: T. Christopher Roth, division partner, Washington Office Building Division, Trammell Crow Company; Dick J. De Beus, chairman of the executive board, Pensionfund PGGM; and Herman A. Vonhof, president, Dutch Institutional Holding Company. (Carol M. Highsmith)

Below: Dedicated in 1987, the Navy Memorial turned out less highfalutin than originally conceived. (Carol M. Highsmith)

Opposite below: Market Square proposal of 1985. (Photo by Harlan Hambright & Associates)

Fourteen years after the 1974 PADC plan was approved, the organization had not opened a single unit of housing. But work was proceeding on renovating Lansburgh's department store and adding an adjacent building for a project that would include 369 loft-like housing units, a theater, and performing-arts space. The Avenue's "critical mass" of housing, though, will be concentrated around Market Square, midway down the Avenue, where a newly created neighborhood, far more open than the old Hill Town, was set to rise on both sides of Eighth Street surrounding the Navy Memorial. The twin, thirteen-story neoclassical towers of the $230 million Market Square project, designed by Hartman-Cox, were built on the last developable site on Pennsylvania Avenue. The project became a reality when Trammell Crow Company of Dallas and the Dutch Institutional Holding Company of Atlanta joined Western Development Corporation and Kan Am Realty in 1987. The tiered top floors of the towers—with the most commanding view of the Mall—were set aside for 225 upscale housing units, each with a balcony. The separate Market Square North, developed by Kingdon Gould, Jr., and incorporating two additional towers, earmarked 201 housing units behind Market Square as well. There's one more piece to the district: Pennsylvania Plaza, developed by the Siegal/Zuckerman/Abernathy/Ruben Partnership.

According to Trammell Crow partner T. Christopher Roth:

Market Square will revive the best features of a nineteenth-century neighborhood, especially the sense of openness and commotion that were so much a part of Center Market and the Market Space retail core. The mixture of Market Square residents and their guests, the project's retail customers, visitors to the Navy Memorial and Archives, combined with those on an "arts walk" from the Smithsonian museums to the National Portrait Gallery will provide a kind of urban energy long dormant on the Avenue.

"Housing is still a question mark for the Avenue," admitted PADC Chairman Berliner, "although [in 1988] there are 350 names, of which mine is one, on a sign-up list to the Market Square developers. The original proposal was 1,500 units in the eastern sector, and it was downsized to 1,200. But I will not be satisfied just to see the 1,200. I want to restore the goal that the original plan had in it, which was 1,500 units."

PADC Executive Director Brodie, who Berliner said was hired over a slew of applicants specifically because of his experience with Baltimore's Housing and Community Development agency, agreed with those who say housing cannot be forced on an area but argued that it made sense as part of the Pennsylvania Avenue experience. "Not to say that cities without downtown housing are immoral or illegal," he said, "but I do think there is a case to be made that they are certainly less exciting, less animated. There is a sense of roots that people put down in the neighborhood that is different from where they work. So I think it's wise that we have persisted with the housing goal in our plan. And we have a wonderful advantage. You can walk up to Congress, walk to the National Gallery of Art. And Pennsylvania Avenue is a fine address."

Above: The Canadian Chancery is one of three buildings on the Avenue to be designed by winners of the Gold Medal from the American Institute of Architects. (Carol M. Highsmith)

Opposite: The Chancery won immediate praise from *Washington Post* architecture critic Benjamin Forgey: "[It] is a mighty battleship of a building with a sharp prow aimed across the wide street at one of the angles of I. M. Pei's National Gallery East. . . . Behind the prow is a great rotunda in the open air, its 12 concrete columns — one for each of Canada's provinces and two territories — echoing the rounded classical revival terminus of the nearby Federal Trade Commission. . . . [Arthur Erickson's] building is an edgy, flawed masterpiece . . . but a masterpiece." (Carol M. Highsmith)

Americans were not the only ones to think so. One day in 1976, Pete Quesada got a phone call from Canadian government officials that, more than any other single event, may have jump-started the Pennsylvania Avenue Development Corporation into measurable accomplishment. "They said, 'Can we send about six men down to talk about putting a chancery on Pennsylvania Avenue?'" Quesada reported.

I knew that some people might object to a foreign government's having a facility on this noble street that we had been describing [during the U.S. Bicentennial year] as an Avenue of America, and that it might create some static. It did, but very little. When the deal got closer, several people from Congress asked me about it. I said, fine, the Canadians are our best friends, and for them to have enough confidence to build this chancery, to me, is very encouraging. We negotiated and negotiated, and in fact it got done.

The Canadians had their eye on square 491, an unrenowned trapezoid surrounded by the Avenue, Sixth Street, C Street, and John Marshall Place. On the southeast corner stood a sixty-one-year-old building that once housed the Ford Motor Company assembly plant. Two residences faced C Street. A yellow-limestone building, designed as a public library but grabbed for the war effort and converted to a federal office building, filled the middle of the Pennsylvania Avenue block. The even-drabber D.C. Employment Security Building, which would be the only square 491 structure to survive, held tight to the corner at Sixth and Penn.

Canada's 290 embassy employees had been spread among three buildings, two on Massachusetts Avenue's Embassy Row. Ultimately they got a choice site along the American inaugural route on the last large parcel in PADC territory set aside for "institutional" use. The deal showed perfect reciprocity. Just as the American post in Ottawa sits across from Parliament, the new Canadian Chancery would lie a curling stone's throw from the U.S. Capitol. Everyone waxed favorable about the deal, but it proved tricky. Ben Gilbert, city planning director at the time, remembered later:

The ground was owned by the District of Columbia. The city has a statute that says it can sell its property only at fair market value. It had been appraised at $7 million. The Canadians had $4 million in their budget. PADC badly wanted it to happen. The Canadians said they could pay only $4 million because the setbacks that are part of the PADC plan deprived them of a third of their building. Finally PADC said it would pay for the setback and threw $2 million into the pot, bringing the price up to $6 million. That left us a million short.

Our negotiating team went into the hall, and I turned to Lou Robbins, who was the [D.C.] corporation counsel, and I said, "Can you live with it? Can you legally justify 6 [million]?" because we wanted it to happen, too. And Lou turned to Sam Starobin and said, "Sam, can you defend this as a reasonable price?" And Sam said, "Yes, I guess so." Three little words: "I guess so," and the deal was done.

The Canadians wasted no time sticking a staff and flag into the vacant lot behind the old "library" building. Passersby "must have wondered why a maple leaf was flying there," mused the *New York Times*.

The architectural commission was won by Arthur Erickson of Toronto, an American Institute of Architects Gold Medalist. Erickson had to design a building, complete with art gallery and public theater, that would complement the National Gallery's modernist East Building, catercorner across the Avenue. The architect failed, *Times* critic Paul Goldberger proclaimed. Erickson instead designed, he said, a "curiously convoluted structure . . . unlikely to fit into the avenue's architectural context." Not that the Avenue had much context. But most other reaction was favorable to Erickson's airy, $30 million building that perches far back from the Avenue. Said Washington's Hugh Newell Jacobsen, "It took the Canadians to finally 'say' something on the north side." Left hunkering next door, looking squat and frowzy, was the old Employment Security Building. It "said" something, too, about the Avenue's all-too-recent days.

Vice President George Bush and Canadian Prime Minister Brian Mulroney attended the 1988 dedication of the $30 million Canadian Chancery, designed by Toronto architect Arthur Erickson, a recipient of the Gold Medal, the highest honor from the American Institute of Architects. (Carol M. Highsmith)

WITNESSES TO THE PASSING OF TIME

Proud as a Peacock Again

Nathaniel Hawthorne, the American author and observer of life's passing parade, always stayed at Willard's hotel when he went to Washington. He said it could "more justly be called the center of Washington and the nation than either the Capitol or the White House, or the State Department." There, he raved, "you mix with office seekers, wire pullers, inventors, artists, poets, editors, Army correspondents, attachés of foreign journals; long-winded talkers, clerks, diplomats, mail contractors, railway directors — until your identity is lost among them!" Willard's was where the word "lobbyist" was said to have been coined for the influence-seekers bending Ulysses S. Grant's ear over a good Havana cigar.

The list of the nation's prominent who did *not* stay at the Willard seemed shorter than that of those who did. Charles Dickens; the Marquis de Lafayette; "Swedish Nightingale" Jenny Lind and her manager, Phineas T. Barnum, certainly did; so did Julia Ward Howe, who, having been asked by a traveling companion to improve upon the morbid words of "John Brown's Body," wrote "The Battle Hymn of the Republic" while Union troops drilled along the Avenue below. Notables were advised to use the Willard's F Street entrance, outsmarting gawking crowds on the Avenue side. Mark Twain, who wrote two books at the Willard, delighted in scurrying out one entrance, in the other, a step ahead of admirers. The first moving picture shown in Washington, called the "Cinematographie Lumiere," was offered at Willard's in 1897.

Henry Willard had been a steamship porter when, in 1847, a wealthy passenger, Benjamin Ogle Tayloe, plucked him off board to try his hand at running Tayloe's row-house City Hotel on Pennsylvania Avenue. So successful was young Willard that he soon leased, and eventually bought, the place and ran his own hotel. In 1900, Willard's nephew, Captain Joseph E. Willard, engaged the architect of New York's Plaza Hotel, Henry Janeway Hardenbergh, to design a beaux-arts "sky-scraper" replacement for the old hotel. Critics greeted it with applause—well-connected guests with their continued patronage. Bandleader Meyer Davis got his start at the Willard in 1919, serenading diners from a golden bridge above the hotel's lavish indoor promenade, Peacock Alley. An advertisement of the 1930s informed the public that

THE WILLARD SERVED
AS THE OFFICIAL WHITE HOUSE
WHEN PRESIDENT AND MRS. COOLIDGE
LIVED HERE FOR A MONTH
DURING HIS ADMINISTRATION
SINGLE ROOMS WITH BATH $4 UP;
DOUBLE ROOMS WITH BATH $6 UP.
THE WILLARD HOTEL,
"RESIDENCE OF PRESIDENTS"

Coolidge had also lived there during his entire vice presidency, but "Residence of Vice Presidents" did not quite have the same ring. The hotel had the city's first "girl bell captain" and a separate ladies' entrance on Fourteenth Street. Hotel bellhops told of slipping guests bottles during Prohibition, ogling a honeymoon couple too preoccupied to draw the drapes, and watching Blackstone the Magician snatch FDR's wallet under the noses of federal agents. Venerable liquor distributor Milton Kronheim said you'd "arrived" when you had your hair cut at the Willard. People who wanted the "right address" had their mail sent to the hotel.

Pages 158–159: The October 8, 1889, parade of the Knights Templar, a Masonic order, was one of the biggest ever in Washington. This view also shows D Street, which was erased for construction of the FBI Building. (Frank Wright)

Opposite: Henry Augustus Willard and Caleb Clapp Willard as young men in 1860. Henry was a bootstrap type who started out as a steamship porter. (James M. Goode Collection, Library of Congress)

Above: President Pierce leaves Willard's in 1853. Here the term "lobbyist" was coined for the loitering influence-seekers *(left)* who later would bend Ulysses S. Grant's ear over a good cigar. (Columbia Historical Society)

161

Right: "The gallant effort of Ellsworth's Zouaves in their successful endeavor to save Willard's Hotel," an 1861 woodcut. The Zouaves were Civil War volunteers for the North who adopted the dress and drill of Algerian infantry who fought under the French flag. (Kiplinger Collection)

Below: The New Willard rose in 1901. During the fight to save the venerable hotel in the 1970s, many members of Congress rose to argue that to level a building where Lincoln had slept was unthinkable. "We certainly weren't about to correct them," said one preservationist. (Culver Pictures)

Above: The Palm Court in 1901, complemented by a lavish indoor arcade dubbed Peacock Alley. It was the archive of early photos by Frances Benjamin Johnston that allowed much of the restoration to be so exacting. (Frances Benjamin Johnston Collection, Library of Congress)

Left: The new lobby seemed commodious enough to live in. Some pretended to do just so. To achieve "the right address," they had their mail sent to the Willard. (Frances Benjamin Johnston Collection, Library of Congress)

Above: A Willard suite *(left)* during the era when Calvin Coolidge, seen in this period caricature *(right)*, set up temporary residence. (Library of Congress)

Left: Perhaps no one wanted to stay at the Willard in the sixties because one would stick to the plastic-looking furniture. The hotel closed in 1968. (Carol M. Highsmith Collection)

Opposite: The second annual Washington Redskins banquet seemed to feature real American Indians in the orchestra. Sentiment for banquets, proms, and weddings held at the Willard helped save the structure. About fifteen members of Congress recalled coming to Washington during World War II and staying at "the grand, old Willard." (Washingtoniana Division, D.C. Public Library)

The hotel lost its strut after World War II, however, as the New Willard began to show wrinkles, got its first owners from outside the family, and faced a hard run from the newer Mayflower, Statler Hilton, and Shoreham uptown. In 1961 Charles B. Benenson and another partner bought the hotel, just as John F. Kennedy was inaugural-riding and directing an Avenue facelift. Two presidential commissions that followed swept away the Willard, on paper, as part of their plans for a great National Square. Benenson and GSA officials discussed swapping sites — the government getting the Willard, Benenson Miller Airfield on Long Island, but Congress scotched the deal. Amid rumors of its demise and the squalor that began to surround it on the Avenue, business dried to a trickle. On July 15, 1968, Benenson closed the hotel, allowing its continued use, however, by the United Citizens for Nixon-Agnew campaign headquarters.

A stubborn (others said eccentric) journalist who lived at the hotel, Trude Feldman, White House correspondent for the *Jewish Press*, moved from room to room, ahead of the shutting off of water and electricity, refusing to leave. Hotel managers did not evict her because she had arranged an interview in the hotel with candidate Richard Nixon. Feldman remained in the hotel, however, the only guest in 449 rooms, for more than two weeks after the interview was completed. "I've had my office here as well as lived here for two years," she told the *Washington Daily News*. "I just can't move so quickly." She became "combination desk clerk, housekeeper and guest, emptying ash trays in the offices, keeping the mirror in the sixth-floor hall polished and answering the red 'reservations' phone in the lobby." *Life* interviewed her; she was taped for the "Today" show. She took her meals at an all-night drugstore on K Street; security guards let her come and go. Feldman left for good a week later when she flew to Miami to cover the Republican National Convention.

The Willard's furniture and fixtures were sold at auction — more like a mob dash for discounts — in 1969. Browsers pried off wallpaper as a souvenir. While the building stood empty, Benenson laid plans to raze it and turn it into an office building. The Fine Arts Commission, anticipating the National Square development, turned him down. There followed Byzantine negotiations, court hearings, legal motions by aroused preservationists, and eventually, plans by the new PADC to save the Willard as a demonstration of its "public-private partnership." Benenson argued that his property had been "constructively taken" by the government, while he still held ownership, by the prolonged denials of his plans to level the building.

Even though he headed the government's PADC, Chairman Quesada agreed with Benenson. "I told him, 'Look, they have deprived you of the use of the land, so the government has in fact already taken it from you,'" Quesada recalled many years later.

He had buyers, but they wouldn't let him sell it. They threatened to take it away from him if he tried to sell it. I said, "Take it to the Court of Claims, and they'll honor your claims." He was encouraged by that. He went to the Court of Claims and won. The court said, yes, the government had taken the property at this date certain, and said it would decide at a later date what damages had accrued to the owners. I was a supporter of the view that it was their private property. There were no limitations on it. The [PADC] plan did not exist, and they had a right of use of it as they saw fit, so long as it conformed to zoning. They wanted to build an office building there, and I resisted emotionally any concept that they should be prevented from doing it. But other [legal] things overtook that.

Quesada's deputy Peter Meszoly remembered things somewhat differently. "I felt that this was really *not* a case of constructive taking and in fact was Benenson's business decision after 1968 not to rehabilitate the hotel [thus lowering its value] that put him in the position that he was in." Once PADC lined up behind saving the Willard, Meszoly said, "We started calling it the 'crown jewel,' using it as leverage to get PADC's funding moving on the Hill. The general didn't care a fig about the Willard at first, but at the end, he, like Nat Owings [whose plans had first proposed demolishing it], thought it was terrific."

After initially thinking that "saving the Willard was a lot of nonsense," General Quesada "found out, when he went up to the Hill to talk about his budget, that the only thing [Representative] Sid Yates and the others on the appropriations committee wanted to talk about was the Willard," said Ben Gilbert. "And he suddenly realized that if he would embrace the Willard, that they wouldn't slash the rest of his plan. He got the whole thing approved. So the plan saved the Willard, but the Willard saved the plan."

In 1975, a bizarre twist was added when a group calling itself the National American Indian Council, or informally, the Thirteenth Indian Tribe, called a news conference to announce it had saved the Willard and bought the hotel. "They were some consortium of unstructured tribes," recalled Frank H. Rich. The Indians never came through with cash to owner Benenson, and, after several Indian leaders listed as board members of the organization told the press they were "shocked" to hear of it, talk of Indians buying the Willard faded into lore.

Finally, after last-ditch court motions to stop demolition, filed by Don't Tear It Down and F Street shoe-store owner Rich, Benenson and PADC agreed on a settlement. Rich remembered one of the court hearings:

[After joining Leila Smith and Don't Tear It Down in taking Benenson to court] I had no financial interest in any of this except the future of my business on F Street. We had to get to court immediately, or forget it. Judge William Jones issued a temporary restraining order, ordering a full hearing. Come the day of the hearing, you have to picture this scene. There were four players: the corporation counsel for the District, my lawyer, the owners' lawyer, and all of a sudden up pops one of the deputy assistant attorneys-general of the United States. Judge Jones was a man of few words, very tough. He started with the corporation counsel — they were lined up like tin soldiers. And he said, "Sir, I want to ask you a question. You've been given an order to tear this building down, and I've given you an order not to tear it down. What are you going to do about this?"

The guy answered, "Your honor, you've given me a problem."

Jones said, "You don't have a problem. All you have to decide is whether you want to go to D.C. Jail or the federal lock-up [if you don't follow the court order]."

Then he went to the representative of the Attorney General of the United States. He said, "I would like to know why the Attorney General has not become interested in this case, since the hotel is under the jurisdiction of the Pennsylvania Avenue Development Corporation." This young man started backing and filling. Jones cut him off. "I've heard all I want to hear," he said. "The government will have to decide whether it wants to be a plaintiff or a defendant by Friday. I'm ordering the government into the case."

Opposite: The hotel ten years after its doors were sealed resembled "the ruins of the Baths of Caracalla." (Carol M. Highsmith)

Below: In the Willard lobby and Peacock Alley, restoration was meticulous. (Carol M. Highsmith)

Ten years after the hotel had closed, PADC got title, Benenson got $4.5 million from PADC (and a like amount later in damages from the Court of Claims) for a hotel for which he had paid $3 million, and the Willard was saved.

PADC officials said they were then astounded to have nine top-notch developers bid on a prospectus to restore and preserve the building. In December 1978, the combination of Stuart S. Golding and the Fairmont Hotel Corporation was chosen to develop the hotel. Delays ensued as the developers encountered high interest rates in securing financing — and strong competition from the new J. W. Marriott Hotel across Fourteenth Street on the Avenue. Eventually Golding turned the bulk of development rights over to a former competitor, the Oliver T. Carr Company, and Fairmont backed away in favor of the worldwide Inter-Continental Hotels chain; Carr won approval to decrease the hotel size and add an office component. Much work was needed.

Interior designer Sarah Tomerlin Lee of New York viewed the vacant and boarded up hotel in 1983 and said it resembled "the ruins of the Baths of Caracalla." Columns and mosaic floors had been eaten away, coffered ceilings were destroyed by water damage, rats the size of cats frolicked in Peacock Alley, and holes in the walls were so enormous, she said, "you could see the cars go by." Meticulous renovation for what had passed for a skyscraper in the squat capital city began in 1984. It was possible only with the aid of 1901 photographs by Frances Benjamin Johnston. Beneath a fluttering sign reading THE WILLARD IS BACK, the lavishly restored and reappointed "crown jewel of Pennsylvania Avenue" was reopened, amid florid reminiscing, in 1986.

John Fondersmith of the city's planning office would look back on the saving of the Willard. "More than anything else," he said, "What killed the earlier Pennsylvania Avenue plans [before PADC] was concern about losing the Willard. There must have been ten or fifteen congressmen get up on the floor and speak against the plan and in favor of saving the Willard. Almost every one of them said he had come to Washington with his family during the war and had stayed at the grand, old Willard."

Ernest Connally of Interior shared the recollection, noting that the Willard of today is an early twentieth-century structure: "People in Congress were scandalized at the thought of destroying the Willard. They thought that Lincoln had stayed in that building. They were out making speeches about this great building that went back to 1840. We certainly weren't about to correct them."

167

Opposite: Pershing Park in bloom opens up a view of the Willard, a site on which a hostelry has stood since 1816. (Carol M. Highsmith)

Above: Lobby of the revived Willard features columns done in scagliola method, a way of imitating marble with tinctured plaster. (Carol M. Highsmith)

Left: A view from a round window in the Willard's mansard roof. (Carol M. Highsmith)

169

Cheating the Wrecker's Ball

Four other historic structures, three once earmarked for destruction as part of one grand redesign or another — and the other the latest in a series of splendid theaters — survive along the Avenue.

The four-story, renaissance-revival Sears House, at 625 Pennsylvania Avenue, was home to the National Photographic Art Gallery of Mathew Brady from 1858 to 1881. In it, Brady's glass-plate photographs caught Abraham Lincoln and many other prominent national leaders. "Every Style of PORTRAIT, from smallest locket size to THE FULL SIZE OF LIFE," read a Brady advertisement. Natural light was vital in photography's primitive days, and Brady — as had four daguerreotypists before him — enjoyed the building's skylights. Perhaps he asked his neighbors, the owners of the adjoining Saint Marc Hotel, if he could set up in their window; from there, or his own vantage point, he shot some of the earliest photos of Center Market and the Washington Mall.

Gilman's Drug Store, Central National Bank, various cigar stores, and the Atlantic Lunch Room were, over time, tenants of the three joined structures in the six hundred block. It was the bank that commissioned A. B. Mullett to add the distinctive turrets in 1887, six years after Brady had left. Between the towers in the 1920s loomed one of the Avenue's best-known displays: the National Soda Cracker Company's Uneeda Biscuit sign. When Gilman's closed in 1967 after 124 years in operation, it was the oldest drugstore in the United States. In 1980, when PADC bought the site for renovation, the Fraternal Order of Police was using the "Brady part" of the building, Mark Weiss camera store another portion, and — best-remembered of all — Apex Liquor Store the rest.

Left: Alfred Mullett's stately towers were bridged by a "Uneeda Biscuit" sign in this 1925 view. The "biscuits" were square soda crackers, similar to unsalted saltines. (Columbia Historical Society)

Above: The interior of Gilman's Drug Store survived intact until 1967, when it was recorded by the Historic American Buildings Survey. (Photo by George Eisenman, James M. Goode Collection, Library of Congress)

171

Above: Sears House in 1975, when it was still known as Apex Liquors. The Fraternal Order of Police was ensconced in the "Brady portion" of the building. Mark Weiss's camera store had replaced Gilman's. (PADC)

Left: Lincoln in a portrait by Mathew Brady. Best known as a chronicler of the Civil War, Brady also recorded Washington society in his Avenue studio into his nineties. His advertisement of 1860 read: "Imperial photographs of all the Presidents from Jackson to Buchanan . . . The colored photographs must be seen to be appreciated . . . One hundred photographs for $5." (National Portrait Gallery)

Right: Along with the Willard Hotel, Sears House is probably the most important private restoration on the Avenue. (Carol M. Highsmith)

Top: One of the many National Theatres. This was Grover's National, named for its manager, Leonard Grover. This National opened on April 22, 1862, and burned on January 28, 1873. When the Civil War ended, gas jets atop the theater spelled out VICTORY. (National Theatre Archives)

Bottom: Don't be fooled by the festive look of this National Theatre premiere. The date was October 13, 1948, and the National was reopening as a movie house. It had closed as a legitimate theater to defray public pressure to integrate its audience. The remodeling job was a garish one. (National Theatre Archives)

The National Theatre building, shoehorned midway along the north side of the 1300 block, has itself not yet marked a century. The current National is the fifth theater on the spot, the four previous having each been destroyed by fire. When it was Grover's National Theatre during the Civil War, Leonard Grover welcomed Abraham Lincoln more than a hundred times. The first National was founded in 1835 by William Corcoran and others, and its patrons have included every U.S. president since that time. Two Washington entrepreneurs rebuilt the theater in 1850 — it had first burned five years earlier — in readiness for Jenny Lind's grand tour of America. The National's most recent renovation in 1984 — after the building was saved from extinction under sweeping National Square designs and incorporated into the larger National Place mixed-use development — uncovered classical medallions and plasterwork that had been painted over in an earlier "modernization." Ben Gilbert recalled when the National Theatre, which once had a "gallery for people of color," . . . declined to allow blacks into the audience.

It was a peculiarity of Washington that the DAR Constitution Hall would not allow blacks to perform on stage, but would allow them in the audience; the National Theatre would permit them on stage, but wouldn't allow them in the audience: a commentary on the illogic of segregation. The National refused to change after the war. It was 1947 when the issue was joined. Richard Coe, the *Post*'s theater critic, led a campaign to open the seats to blacks, the owner refused to do it and [in 1948, following a performance of *Oklahoma!*] converted the place into a movie theater. Civic pressure four years later resulted in new owners taking it over and opening it on an integrated basis.

The list of stars that have performed at the National deserves (and has) a book of its own.

The beaux-arts Evening Star Building, whose naked facade fascinated passersby for two years while PADC-approved renovations gutted its interior at Eleventh Street, was built in 1899. It housed the city's "establishment" newspaper until 1958, then Justice Department tenants. The ornate, unairconditioned building was uncomfortable, former reporter Bill MacDougall told the *Washington Times*. Electric fans were not permitted in the newsroom and composing room, MacDougall said, because they blew papers about. The building did feature two novel devices: a machine in the basement that circulated ice water — helpful where brows were sweating — and a system that rang a bell in the newsroom whenever a fire alarm sounded anywhere in the District of Columbia.

Above: The Evening Star Building on July 4, 1903, was all dressed up for Independence Day galas. The building proved to be as uncomfortable as it was aesthetic. Electric fans were banned from the newsroom because they blew papers about. (Library of Congress)

Left: Just before the official announcement, this family read all about the Japanese surrender of 1945. The Evening Star Building is in the background. Soon the Avenue would be engulfed in yet another celebration. (National Archives)

Across the Avenue from the spruced-up Star hovers another turn-of-the-century period piece, the 1899 Old Post Office Building, which the *New York Times*, immediately upon the hulking building's opening, called "a cross between a cathedral and a cotton mill." The *Saturday Evening Post* wasn't much kinder in 1929, sneering, "That huge and grotesque pile we call the Post Office Department Building is to go, and will go unmourned."

The city's first steel-frame building, by Supervising Architect of the Treasury Willoughby J. Edbrooke, lasted as a post office only eighteen years. When postal clerks moved to a site next to Union Station, the brooding Old Post Office was used for storage and overflow offices. Many plans called for its destruction. First, during the 1920s, the "old tooth" was marked for extraction as out of step with neoclassical Federal Triangle grandeur. According to Gail Karesh Kassan, Congress refused to condemn it, "even though it was stated that 'the building was very wasteful as to space, perhaps one of the most uneconomical buildings used by the government in the entire country.'"

Come the many blight-fighting Pennsylvania Avenue committees of the 1960s and '70s, the Old Post Office, its weathered facade dark and grimy, seemed doomed again. Avenue planner Owings did assent to retain the 315-foot tower and its ten "Congress bells," duplicative of those in Westminster Abbey in London. The 1964 Avenue council report said the tower could serve "as a memento of the times it represents, as a vertical punctuation of the Avenue, and as a city lookout." But it took a rare majority vote to agree on that stand. A permit was issued for the main building's demolition in 1971, but dogged efforts by Don't Tear It Down and by Nancy Hanks, chairman of the National Endowment for the Arts, saved the structure. Hanks died before the building was rededicated as the Nancy Hanks Center. The first-floor ceiling that blocked the view of the building's neck-craning interior court having been removed, the Old Post Office reopened as a retail pavilion in 1983.

Washington attorney Robert Peck worked for the National Endowment for the Arts in 1974 and was a later president of Don't Tear It Down. He said an unsung hero in saving the Old Post Office was a midlevel GSA bureaucrat who had the papers "authorizing the demolition and buried them on his desk . . . until the demolition storm had passed." A rumor of the time was that the FBI centralized its wiretapping operations somewhere in the building, which at the time was dark, dank, and a perfect setting for an Edward G. Robinson caper. "When

Opposite: Workers gutted the Evening Star in 1987. (Carol M. Highsmith)

Above: A Labor Day parade passes the Old Post Office in the 1890s. (Library of Congress)

the building was saved," added Peck, "I took it as a great irony that some of the first people who wanted into the space were the tax attorneys from the Department of Justice. Tax men in an artsy place! It meant that Pennsylvania Avenue had become a terrific location and that the old place had 'arrived.'"

Above: The Avenue at the turn of the century. Only the Willard, the Old Post Office, and the Capitol dome are extant today. Missing notables include the GAR Building, the Occidental Hotel and Restaurant, Warwick's Billiard Parlors, and the Raleigh Hotel. The tower of the Southern Railway Building partially blocks the Old P.O. An 1897 advertisement called the line, "the great Battlefield Line of the South. More than ninety percent of the battles during the late War between the States were fought on or near the lines of the SOUTHERN RAILWAY." (James M. Goode Collection, Library of Congress)

Right and opposite: Filled with shops, the Old Post Office has provided a bridge to bring tourists from the Mall to the Avenue. (Carol M. Highsmith)

178

Epilogue: Your Main Street

Elbert Peets once wrote about a driven, headstrong master of the planning trade who left an indelible imprint on the capital of the American nation: "His leading mental quality — both a weakness and a strength — was a frenzied desire to do things *en grand*. Indubitably he was erratic. Heroic visions and inexplicable blindness could exist together in him. His stupendous plan is full of exasperating, almost impudently willful, absurdities. His reports reveal an overflowing enthusiasm for his conceptions."

But about whom was Peets writing? It could be either of two men: the enigmatic Frenchman, L'Enfant, or Nathaniel Owings, the brusque champion of the L'Enfant vision through nearly two decades — and three stormy commissions — almost two centuries later.

Son of a French court painter who had depicted many battle scenes, L'Enfant was a child of Versailles. Though he himself would design many fortifications, he was never trained as an engineer. Like his countryman Lafayette, he came to America to raise the democratic revolutionary banner. Wounded, captured, and later exchanged, he worked on forts (underdrawing and overspending, according to architect Donald A. Hawkins, secretary of the L'Enfant Forum, a group of the Frenchman's devotees) and won a promotion. George Washington knew him well, since L'Enfant had illustrated Baron von Steuben's training manuals. And the young Frenchman wrote the great general often, especially as L'Enfant was working on the Federal Hall in New York. Its execution marked the first of many quarrels the arrogant aristocrat would pick with unromantic pragmatists who commissioned him. The first President sent him to the Potomac to survey and design a new capital city. "On the day that L'Enfant submitted his first plan to Washington, Louis XVI, seeking to escape from France, was brought back to Paris," wrote Peets. "The tragic occurrences in his native country added to the strain on L'Enfant; they also reduced him from financial independence to ultimate penury."

In the cowpaths and brambles along the Potomac lowlands, L'Enfant foresaw a city of incomparable scale. Harking back to Versailles and to broad Parisian boulevards, he dashed off epic diagonals, places for monuments, and cooling waterscapes. Frederick Gutheim described him as "first and foremost an artist . . . with the temperament to match." Hawkins said he was "high-strung and talked a lot, but there's not much agreement on anything else," including the looks of the man. Only two silhouettes purporting to depict the quarrelsome planner are known to survive, and neither resembles the other. It's a deficiency that kept L'Enfant's likeness off a U.S. postage stamp.

His drawings do not survive, either; they were stolen out of his quarters, and we are left with interpolations of L'Enfant by the surveyor Andrew Ellicott and others. Since he had left Paris at age twenty-two, he'd not had a chance to travel the Continent widely, but he appeared to have studied the great city plans of Europe. "Notwithstanding I would reprobate the idea of imitating," he wrote Jefferson, "yet the contemplation of what exists of well improved situation, even the parallel of these which defective ones, may serve to suggest a variety of new ideas." In *Cities and People*, Mark Girouard stated that L'Enfant's sketch of Washington "is arguably the most brilliant town plan ever conceived," especially in the relief his diagonals provide from the monotony of the typical American grid." It was an artist's work of art.

"Opinions of L'Enfant the man vary from an absolute genius of landscape planning and design to a luckily placed neurotic dreamer," said Hawkins. In either case, he was a bad match for the rough-hewn time and place in which he practiced. To the notion that the Capitol and President's House were set too far apart to support easy transit of those representing each branch of government, L'Enfant turned imperial. Congress and the president should rarely fraternize, he believed. Messages could be delivered by carriage. It was because he envisioned a "palace" for the president that the axial avenue between two great buildings would have worked as the ceremonial link. Had the White House been built to his scale with its grand entrance to the south or east, and had Mills's Treasury Building not plopped in the way, Pennsylvania Avenue would have run right into a corner of the building. The path that would ultimately front 1600 Pennsylvania Avenue would have been part of a Versailles-like garden out back.

Gutheim wrote of L'Enfant in *Worthy of the Nation* that "his desire for simultaneous development of several districts at once brought him into conflict with President Washington and the commissioners and eventually caused his downfall and his dismissal; the man was rejected, but never his plan." Fearing that speculators would get hold of his plan and drive up the cost of parcels, perhaps compromising one of his precious elements, he hoarded the drawings, even from the city commissioners. Instructed by Washington to hue to their authority, he threw a snit and was fired. He was offered $2,500 for his efforts but refused it as inadequate and insulting.

L'Enfant showed up in New Jersey, of all places, designing the town of Paterson, but Peets reported that the town fathers found his ideas too grandiose. After a Philadelphia client defaulted on a commission, he returned to Washington, where he spent his last years hounding Congress for suitable back payment. Demanding almost one hundred thousand dollars, he got three thousand. According to Peets, "His last year was spent at the home of a country gentleman near Washington."

So it was L'Enfant whom Peets was describing, but it could just as easily have been Owings.

A frenzied desire to do things en grand? "Nat could talk the balls off a brass monkey," remembered Charles Horsky. "Full of enthusiasm, he was willing to work any number of hours and days for his plan. He regarded it as the great effort of his life, and by God, it was going to be good."

Indubitably he was erratic? "Owings was one of those extraordinary men you either absolutely adored and thought everything he did was at least surprising and wonderful or different and difficult, or you just took umbrage at him," said David Childs. "He was gregarious, warm, violent, one of those classical men of power."

Heroic visions and inexplicable blindness could exist together in him? "Nat's romantic vision was very appealing in some ways," recalled Andy Barnes. "But some of his ideas [Barnes mentioned National Square] could be ridiculous. He could be very warm and generous, very mercurial."

His stupendous plan is full of exasperating, almost impudently willful, absurdities? "Without [National Square], the plan is no plan at all," Owings pouted in *Holiday* magazine.

His reports reveal an overflowing enthusiasm for his conceptions? "He was always lobbying for his ideas. He really cared about the [Avenue] plan, but he fought hard for his ideas," said Ben Gilbert from his home in Tacoma. "He was less of a consensus person than he might have been."

Nat Owings had already made a bold mark by the time his attention turned to Pennsylvania Avenue. He built what the *Post*'s Von Eckardt called "the largest yet probably most consistently excellent architectural firm in the country — Skidmore, Owings & Merrill." Owings was not a "design man." He joked within his firm that all he could remember designing were some doorknobs in architecture school. He *did* allow that he'd configured the men's rooms for the Commerce Department Building.

Owings was instead an old-fashioned, self-made entrepreneur and recruiter. He'd been the driving force behind the soaring U.S. Air Force Academy, Baltimore's "design team" that stopped a twelve-lane bridge across the Inner Harbor, and the Cry California campaign that saved the beauty of Big Sur, his home when he got the call from Washington.

Having conspired with Goldberg, Moynihan, and Walton in 1962 to decoy a refurbishing of Pennsylvania Avenue behind a study of federal office space, Fritz Gutheim retired to ponder possible candidates to get the job done. "The next time we met, Moynihan told us that Richard Goodwin at the White House, who was a cultural type, had as his candidate for chairman the German émigré Mies van der Rohe. I knew Mies quite well, and I couldn't imagine anyone less likely to get along with Congress. He was a real autocrat, so at that point I was asked for a nomination, and I suggested Nathaniel Alexander Owings." Everyone soon agreed that he was an inspired choice. "Skid, as I think he called him, and Merrill were dead, and the firm was doing fine," said Moynihan. "This seized him. It became his life."

Owings threw himself into the job, forgetting his manners and often his appearance. He chuckled that it was time to get a new necktie, since his expense account was all over the one he wore. He got his way by bullying and bruising, regaling with stories, sometimes by storming out of the room and threatening to leave talkers and dreamers with real work. He buttonholed members of Congress, snowed reporters, even talked bulldog J. Edgar Hoover into agreeing to a setback for his FBI mausoleum. He championed Thiry's grand plan for a street wall of facades down the north side of the avenue, and of course his own for the National Square, thundering that architecture existed not to create monuments but to frame spaces. He cared not at all what went on *inside* buildings. "Owings' concern was primarily pragmatic," Gutheim remembered. "He wanted to see something built. He was not all that interested in the historic aspects at first [shedding no tears over buildings like the Willard that might have to fall]. Rather it was the grand design, and getting something done." Through it all, he never took a penny for his work on the Avenue.

Owings was a compact, slightly hunched, bullet-shaped man. David Childs, whom Owings recruited as chief designer on Johnson's Temporary Commission, found the native Hoosier a "sixty-five-year-old man talking revolutionary ideas, getting traffic out of cities, wonderful, large-scale concerns about how people would use public spaces. You'd have a room full of forty people — senators, the President of the United States," said Childs,

And when that brawny man with the big hands would walk in, he had the charisma, the force of personality, that he was the center of the room in no time, irritating or amusing you, depending upon whether you could stand up to him. If you got in the way of [his dream for] Pennsylvania Avenue, he was ruthless; he'd roll over you.

But his heart was in the right place. He was not doing it for Nat Owings. He couldn't care less. I remember one night, maybe it was Pat Moynihan saying, "Well, Nat, you'll have your name on one of these streets someday." Nat was totally surprised. He had absolutely no interest in it. He had opposed putting [PADC Chairman] Joe Danzansky's name on the Avenue, said you can't do that for a hundred years, after somebody's dead.

Those who loved him shared a running joke about the perfect Nat Owings Memorial, right on Pennsylvania Avenue: either the Apex Liquor Store or the Cogswell Society's Temperance Fountain, for Owings's visions for the first half of his time on the Avenue were often blurred by the bottle. Pennsylvania Avenue Council members muttered, knowingly, whenever Moynihan would have to "immobilize Nat." Moynihan once guided the architect back to his room at the Hay-Adams, threw him in the shower to sober up, and stole his pants so he'd not embarrass a pending deliberation by showing up. Members were stunned to see Owings burst through the door anyway. He had ordered room service and bought the pants off the waiter.

His "dear, collusive friend" Bill Walton tells a more pitiable tale. "We were having a crucial meeting somewhere in the Smithsonian. It was a public meeting; there would have been public architects there. As I arrived, Moynihan was pacing up and down. He grabbed me and said, 'We're in terrible trouble. I've had to lock Nat in his room. He's falling-down drunk. You'll have to take over as chairman.'

"Well I did. Halfway through, Moynihan and I both happened to look up at the same time. There at the back of the room came Nat Owings, [disheveled], his hair down over his eyes: the worst apparition of an alcoholic I had ever seen in my life. Moynihan, his friend and trooper, very inconspicuously got up and walked in that direction, put his arm around him and got him out." It's variously reported that Moynihan, Owings's second wife Margaret, or someone at SOM took Nat aside and told him he would lose his dream, his involvement in Pennsylvania Avenue, if the drinking continued. Overnight, following the gruelling, Antabuse crash cure on the West Coast, he switched to seltzer water, and, so far as anyone knew, never took a drink again. In 1988, when General Quesada, with whom Owings worked and spatted for three years on the PADC board, was asked about Owings's drinking, he replied with a stunned silence. Quesada had no idea that Nat drank.

Owings's involvement in Washington ended when he demanded of PADC Chairman Max Berry that a board meeting be changed because he, Owings, could not make it. "He used some four-letter words," Berry recalled. "It was shocking. He said, if I was too rude not to reschedule the meeting, he was going to resign. I said, 'Go ahead. Is this oral, or are you going to put this in writing?' He said he'd have my head and have X and Y fire me. He didn't, of course, and he did resign. I am sure some people think I was wrong by not succumbing to him, but I wasn't chairman of PADC to do that."

Nat Owings retired to another city that he loved: Santa Fe. David Childs remembered visiting him a week before Owings died of cancer. "He used to go out and sleep on the ground where corn-dance rituals were performed. He believed in spirits and magic. He talked about his temple, the baking sun. Sitting in his little square, amid his adobe buildings, he came to peace with the world. He'd needed to have time to have closure. People he'd had fights with came back to say good-bye." The American Institute of Architects bestowed its highest honor, its Gold Medal, on Nathaniel Owings shortly before he died.

How faded seem the memories of Owings's time when downtown Washington, like downtown everywhere, seemed moribund, decay having spread to all vital organs of commerce, accommodation, and culture. How we forget, looking down an Avenue of the Presidents made grand again, how dire were those days. Were there really sharpshooters on the roof of every building for Nixon's first inaugural, as there had been for Lincoln's? Could it have been that one of the classiest office addresses in America was once written off as unrentable? Was today's Avenue of skaters and theater parties and promenading diplomats once, a bare decade or so ago, a row of unremitting porn to the north and castles of scorn to the south? It was.

The Avenue today is powdered and pressed and all dressed up for a world to come see. One nagging question, one stray thread out of place, remains. Is there yet *real* life on the great ceremonial way? Housing will help answer in the affirmative. So will artists, drifting down from Seventh Street — if the planners of such well-groomed urban space can take a scruffy poet mixed with scrubbed tourists and marching bands. Life won't have to be induced on an Avenue that, like Dorothy's tin man, has found its heart; we won't again need National Breakdance Contests on Freedom Plaza or the Fast Flying Festibules at Market Square to draw a crowd. Just look at those old photos: Great places are their own attraction.

John Woodbridge, one of the first voices crying in an urban wasteland, saw not just Nat Owings and Pete Quesada, Max Berry and Hank Berliner — but also unsung tulip planters and building painters, checkers-players and streetlamp changers — turn an embarrassment into a showpiece. "These things don't happen in this country with grand, autocratic gestures," Woodbridge said. "They happen by accretion. Like the piecemeal additions to the U.S. Capitol over a couple of centuries, they can add up to something wonderful, even when not all the pieces are that wonderful." The whole of the revitalized Main Street of America can be more than its parts.

Nat Owings would probably have ultimately agreed, were he with us, that to have knocked down all the old places with character — the Post Office tower, the turrets at Sears, the old Willard, the Star — would have brought symmetry but torn out the Avenue's heart. We'd have had dignity, but not grace. Too many "shopping experiences" on the Avenue are indoors still, too many "events" pre-planned, too many guests seeing the expanse on twenty-minute parole off a bus from Great Bend. But slowly, by *accretion*, life, daytime and nighttime life, is cracking through Mellon's Great Wall. The Pennsylvania Avenue Development Corporation found out that buildings alone can't attract it, and drafting-board plans most certainly cannot. Parade life falls away with the last bass drum. Odd little shops and wonderful smells, places for young ones to run and old ones to rest while surveying the passing scene bring life. Pennsylvania Avenue — The Avenue, your Main Street — is getting there.

Suggested Reading List

Personal interviews produced a wealth of information about the recent (JFK and beyond) history of Pennsylvania Avenue. The serious student of the Avenue and its place in American history is advised to plumb carefully magazine articles, Washington newspapers, and the *New York Times*, for the subject is but lightly brushed in most of the books on the nation's capital. Well worth searching out, however, are the bound reports of the four commissions that rethought the Avenue: The Ad Hoc Committee on Federal Office Space (1962), the President's Council on Pennsylvania Avenue (1964), the Temporary Commission on Pennsylvania Avenue (1968), and the Pennsylvania Avenue Plan of the Pennsylvania Avenue Development Corporation (1974). The last of these reports was revised by PADC in "Amendments to the Pennsylvania Avenue Plan" (1986). PADC annual reports are also laden with historical and modern photographs, maps, and building descriptions.

Not all books that touch on the Avenue are recommended, since some seem so cursory or hastily assembled as to be of shaky reliability. Among outstanding works worth studying, however, are:

Bryan, Wilhelmus Bogart. *A History of the National Capital*. New York City: Macmillan Company, 1914.

Cable, Mary. *The Avenue of the Presidents*. Boston: Houghton Mifflin Company, 1969.

Durban, Louise. *Inaugural Cavalcade*. New York City: Dodd, Mead & Company, 1971.

Eskew, Garnett Laidlaw. *Willard's of Washington*. New York: Coward-McCann, Inc., 1954.

Goode, James M. *Capital Losses: A Cultural History of Washington's Destroyed Buildings*. Washington, D.C.: Smithsonian Institution Press, 1979.

Goode, James M. *The Outdoor Sculpture of Washington, D.C.* Washington, D.C.: Smithsonian Institution Press, 1974.

Gutheim, Frederick. *The Federal City: Plans and Realities*. Washington, D.C.: Smithsonian Institution Press, 1981.

Gutheim, Frederick (consultant), National Capital Planning Commission. *Worthy of the Nation: The History of Planning for the National Capital*. Washington, D.C.: Smithsonian Institution Press, 1977.

Hines, Christian. *Early Recollections of Washington City*. Reprint. Washington, D.C.: Junior League of Washington, 1981.

Hines, Thomas H. *Burnham of Chicago*. New York: Oxford University Press, 1974.

Junior League of Washington. *The City of Washington: An Illustrated History*. New York: Alfred A. Knopf, 1985.

Kelly, Charles S. *Washington, D.C., Then and Now: Before and After D.C.* New York: Dover Publications Inc., 1984.

King, LeRoy O., Jr. *100 Years of Capital Traction: The Story of Streetcars in the Nation's Capital*. Self-published, 1972.

Lee, Richard M. *Mr. Lincoln's City*. McLean, Virginia: EPM Publications, Inc., 1981.

Leech, Margaret. *Reveille in Washington, 1860-1865*. New York: Harper & Brothers, 1942.

Moore, Charles. *Daniel H. Burnham: Architect, Planner of Cities*. Boston: Houghton Mifflin Company, 1921 (two volumes).

Peets, Elbert. *On the Art of Designing Cities: Selected Essays of Elbert Peets*. Cambridge: MIT Press, 1968.

Proctor, John Claggett. *Washington Past and Present*. New York: Lewis Historical Publishing Company, 1930.

Reed, Robert. *Old Washington, D.C. in Early Photographs*. Mineola, New York: Dover Publications, Inc., 1980.

Topham, Washington. *First Railroad Into Washington and Its Three Depots*. Records of the Columbia Historical Society, March 20, 1923.

United States Department of the Interior. *The Pennsylvania Avenue District in United States History*, a "Report on the National Significance of Pennsylvania Avenue and Historically Related Environs," Washington, D.C., 1965.

Wiebenson, John. *Replanning Pennsylvania Avenue*. Washington, D.C. 1971.

Young, James Sterling. *The Washington Community 1800-1828*. New York: Columbia University Press, 1966.

Index

References to photograph captions
are *italicized*.

Acme Liquor Store. 84

Adams, John. 75

Ad Hoc Committee on Federal Office
Space. 8, 11, 122

Agriculture, Department of. 39

Albee Building. 86

Alcohol, Tobacco and Firearms,
Bureau of. 27

Alex, Bill. 126

Allen, Roy. 124

Al's Magic Shop. *120,* 121

American Cities Building. 26, 147

American Colonization Society and
hall. 40

American Institute of Architects. *40,*
104, 105, *154,* 184

American Security Bank Building. 19

Anacostia River. *See* Eastern Branch

Apex Building. *See* Federal Trade
Commission Building

Apex Liquors. 39, *65, 78,* 116, 120, 171,
172, 183

Arches: Garfield, *90,* 91; Pershing, *96,*
96; Navy Memorial, 143, *143*

Archihorse. 143, *143*

Architects and architecture. 8, 108,
133, 142, 143, 151

Ariel Rios Building. 27

Arlington Memorial Bridge. 64,
104–105

Arthur, Chester A. *88*

Arts and artists: add life, 184;
district, 137; walk, 153; like wine
with a meal, 142

Asbill, Mac, Jr. *144,* 145

Atlantic Coast Line Building. 39

Atlantic Lunch Room. 171

Atzerodt, George. 31

Avenue Associates Limited
Partnership. 37

Avenue House Hotel. 39

Avenue Souvenir Shop. 120

B Street. 62–64. *See also* Constitution
Avenue

Baltimore & Ohio Railroad. *See*
Railroads

Baltimore & Potomac Railroad. *See*
Railroads

Bank Square. 77

Barnes, W. Anderson "Andy." 117, 134,
136–137, 182

Barney's. *See* Susser

Barnum, Phineas T. 160

Barry, Marion, Jr. 130

Battle Hymn of the Republic, The. 14,
160

Be Kind to Animals parade. *94*

Benenson, Charles B. 10, 165–166

Berliner, Henry A., Jr. 13, 131, *134,*
137, 146, 147, 153, 184

Berry, Max N. 128, 142, 145, 147, 184

Bible, Alan. 117, 131

Bicentennial, U.S. 133,154

Blackstone the Magician. 24, *24,* 160

Bladensburg, Maryland: stage stop,
67; turnpike, 75

Blue Book report. 127

Board of Trade, Greater Washington.
146

Bonus March. 96, *99*

Bookmaking. 120

Booth, John Wilkes. 14, 31, *31,* 40, *82*

Boston Dry Goods. 35, *76,* 77

Braddock's Rock. 61, 64

Brady, Mathew: imagined, 117; studio,
19, 39, 120, 171, *172;* portraits, *63,*
172

Brice, Fanny. 118

British burning of Washington, *21,* 23,
23, 43, 113, 115

Britten, Fred. 71

Broadcast News movie. 32, *32*

Brodie, M.J. "Jay".128, 137, 142, 147,
153

Brothels. 61, *106*

Brown, Glenn. 105

Brown, J. Carter. 40, *40, 111,* 113

Brown's Indian Queen Hotel. 39, *53,* 67

Brunswick, Hotel. 44, *44*

Buchanan, James. *40, 88,* 89, *90,* 91

Burger, Warren. 118

Burgunder, B. Bernei, Jr. 116

Burnes, David. 51, 61

Burnham, Daniel. 61, 68, 104, *105*

Burroughs, John. *44*

Buttell, Louis G. 100

C&P Telephone, Washington
Company, 146, *147*

Cabot, Cabot and Forbes. 27

Cadillac-Fairview Company. 32

Canadian Chancery. 14, 40, 137, 145,
154, 154–156, *156*

Canals: C&O, 69; City, 50, *54,* 61, 62,
63; vestige, *65*

Cannon, Joseph. 23, 105, 131

Canterbury Hotel. 35, *76*

Capitol, U.S.: additions, 184; British
burn, *23, 43;* cornerstone, 55;
distance from White House, 181;
during '68 riots, 115; impressions of,
42, 61; reflecting pool, 44, 133; at
sunset, *46;* views and vista, 19, 40,
53, 55, *105;* Western Plaza model,
130, *130, 136;* winter at, *58. See also*
Congress House

Capitol Hill: cascade, 61; rails near
and across, *66,* 67, 71; Tiber course
through, 61

Carr, Oliver T. 166

Carter, Jimmy. 86, *87,* 91, 100

Carter, Rosalynn. 100, *100*

Carusi's dancing saloon. 81

Cassatt, Alexander. 68

Center Leg Freeway. 44, 128

Center Market: befouling of, 62;
comfort station, 39, *39;* commerce
around, 77; fire, 64; one-stop
shopping center, 75–77; pavilion, 39;
views, *38, 75*

Central Building. *82*

Central National Bank. 77, 171

Chalk, O. Roy. 71, *71*

Childs, David. 126, 127, 131, 134, 150,
151, 182, 183, 184

Chinatown. 42, 75

Chyun, Yong-Duk. 135, 136–137,
142–143

City Beautiful movement. 8, 68, 104,
105

Civil War: bodies in Tiber, 62; gaslight
spells victory *174;* guardhouse, 35;

marching, 55, 63, 67, 160; sabotage of trains, *66;* troops discover a delicacy, 84; Zouaves fight Willard fire, *162*

Clay, Henry. 40

Coast Guard Building, U.S. 26

Coe, Richard. 174

Cogswell, Henry. 39

Cogswell Society Temperance Fountain. *35,* 39, 183

Cohen, Al. *120,* 121

Cohen, Richard S. 26, 138, *138*

Commerce Department Building. 24, *24,* 182

Committee of One Hundred. 108

Congress, U.S.: lobbying, 126, 127, 134, 136; opposes Avenue plans, 126–127, 131, 133–134, 145; and PADC, 135–136; passes ICTC, 138; railroads disturb, 67; streetcars annoy, 71; testimony, 126–127, 133, 135; places Treasury Building, 22, 23; and the Willard, 165, 166

Congress House. 13, 50

Connally, Ernest A. 61, 134, 167

Constitution, U.S. 130, 135

Constitution, U.S.S. hull. 91

Constitution Avenue: B Street renamed, 64; covers canal, *54;* suggested inaugural route, 115. *See also* B Street

Coolidge, Calvin. 86, 107, 160, *164*

Cooper, Henry Allen. 64

Corcoran Office Building. 24, 86

Corcoran, William Wilson. 19, 174

Council of Governments. 117

Covington & Burling, Attorneys. 147

Coxey's Army. 95

Cultural center, proposed 1960s. 124. *See also* International Cultural and Trade Center

Custer, George A. *88,* 89

Custis, Washington Parke. 67

D Street. 35, *161*

Danzansky, Joe. 183

DAR Constitution Hall. 174

Dart, Justin. 134

Davidson, Graham. *32*

Davidson, Stephen L. 116, 120–121

Davis, Meyer. 160

De Beus, Dick J. *152*

Depression, Great. 112

Dewey, George. 96, *96*

Dickens, Charles. 160

District Building: described, 26; proposed as opera house, 124; pylons fronting, 130

Don't Tear It Down, Inc. 166, 177

Douglas, Melvyn. 118

Douglass, Frederick. 19

Downtown Progress. 146

Dream Books. 120

Dulles International Airport. 130, 134

Dutch Institutional Holding Company. *152,* 153

E Street. 26, 124, 128

E Street Expressway. 128

Eastern Branch: as Avenue terminus, 51; growth toward, 127; towns on, 50

Ebbitt House. 22, 84

Edbrooke, Willoughby J. 177

Ehrlichman, John. 127

Eighth Street. 37, 151, 153

Eisenhower, Dwight D. 86, *87,* 96

Ellicott, Andrew. 50, *51,* 181

Emergency Hospital. 113

Employment Security Building, D.C. 40, 154, 156

Erickson, Arthur. 154, 156, *156*

Esso Building. 44

Evening Star Building. *28,* 31, 81, 174, 175, 177, 184

F Street. *63,* 81, 115, 128, 160, 166

Fairmont Hotel Corporation. 167

FBI Building: block razed for, *82;* Hoover on, 128; disparaged, 123, 128; exhibits in, 127–128; genesis, 8, 127; located, 35; view, *129*

Federal Bureau of Investigation. 13, 177

Federal City Bicentennial Development Corporation. 133

Federal City Council. 136, 138, 146

Federal Reserve Annex. 141

Federal Trade Commission (Apex) Building. 39, 108, *109, 111,* 113, *154*

Federal Triangle: architecture, 8, 14, 108–112, *109;* as barrier, 138, 184; buildings razed and excavation for, *24,* 39, *39,* 64, 84, *106, 111,* 113; cost, *109,* 112; criticism of, 113; land purchase, 107; Mellon board and construction history, 9, 108–112; parking lot, 10, 11, *113;* squatters in, 96; traffic from, 71; view, *109. See also* Grand Plaza

Feldman, Trude. 165

Fifteenth Street. 14, 22, *23, 24,* 91

Fillmore, Abigail. 88

Fillmore, Millard. 13

Fine Arts Commission. 84, 107, 127, 165

Flanigan, Peter. 127

Fondersmith, John. 115, 127, 135, 167

Ford, Gerald R. 13, 136

Ford, Henry. 40

Ford Motor Company assembly plant. 14, 40, *99,* 154

Forgey, Benjamin. *154*

Forgotten Bungalow. 113

Four-and-one-half Street. 42, *85*

Fourteenth Street. *27, 71*

Frank, Abraham. 13

Frankfurter, Felix. 37

Franklin National Bank. 77

Franklin statue. 14, 31

Freedman's Savings Bank. 19

Freedom Plaza. *See* Western Plaza

French & Richardson bookstore. 35, *35*

Friedberg, M. Paul. *24,* 131

Fritz Reuter, Hotel. *40*

Funerals: F.D.R., *92;* Harrison, 88; Kennedy, *92;* Lincoln, 89, *92;* Unknown Soldier, 96

Gallatin statue. 19

Galt Jewelers. 23

Garfield, James A. 68, *69, 88, 90,* 91

Garner, John Nance. 118

General Services Administration. 123, 126–127, 131, 135, 138, 165. *See also* Golden, Public Buildings Service

George Washington Hotel. 23

Geronimo. *90*

Gilbert, Ben. 115, 127, 151, 154–156, 166, 174, 182

Gilbert, Cass. 107

Gilman's Drugs. 39, *78*, 171, *171*

Goldberg, Arthur J. 121, 122–123, 136, 150, 182

Goldberger, Paul. 156

Golden, Terence. 11

Golding, Stuart S. 167

Goode, James M. 22, 31, 44, 131

Goodwin, Richard. 182

Goose Creek. 61. *See also* Tiber Creek

Goozh, Jean and Gifts. 118

Gould, Kingdon, Jr. 153

Government Financial Operations, Bureau of. 19

Grafly, Charles A. *136*

Grand Army of the Republic: building, 14, 19, 24, *24*, 86, *178;* parade, *88,* 89; statue, 39

Grand Plaza. 112, *113,* 138

Grant, Ulysses S. 13, 160, *161*

Great White City. 104

Green Book report. 124–127

Greenough, Horatio. *44*

Grover's. *See* National Theatre

Guiteau, Charles J. 68, *69*

Gutheim, Frederick. 14, 62, 108, 113, 123, 124, 181, 182–183

Hamilton statue. 19

Hancock statue. 37, *37*

Hancock's Old English Inn. 117

Hanks, Nancy. 177

Hardenbergh, Henry Janeway. *31,* 160

Harding, Warren G. 91, 96, 107

Harrison, Benjamin, *88,* 95

Harrison, William Henry. *53,* 88

Hartman-Cox, Architects. *32,* 153

Harvey's oyster house. 32, 84, *85,* 113

Hash Row. *85*

Haskell, Douglas. 123

Hawkins, Donald A. 61, 181

Hawthorne, Nathaniel. 160

Hay Market. 35, *76*

Hayes, Rutherford B. *88*

Height restrictions. 14, 136

Heurich Building. 27, *96*

Heyburn Plan. 107

Hickman, Beau. 117

Hill Town. *See* Housing

Hines, Christian. 55, 61

Hoban, James. 23, *53*

Hooker, Joseph. 61, *63*

Hooker's Division. 61

Hoover, J. Edgar. 127, 128, *129,* 182

Hope, Bob. 13–14

Horsky, Charles. 117, 121, 126, 127, 182

Houdini, Harry. 23

Housing: as an "Avenue experience," 153; Hill Town, 135, *150,* 151; low-income, 151; Market Square (1980s), 153; Owings's support of, 150; as PADC mission, 137, 151; Temporary Commission plan, 126

Howe, Julia Ward. 160

"I Have a Dream" speech. 13, 14

Inaugurals: described, *40,* 86–100, 184; extemporaneous fun, 86; Kennedy's spurs Avenue rebirth 14, 121–122; symbolism, 122; views, *82, 87, 88, 90, 99;* watching, 86

Indiana Plaza, *39,* 53

Indians, American. 42, *43, 90, 91, 135, 164,* 166

Interior Department survey. 138

Internal Revenue Service Building. 32, 112

International Cultural and Trade Center. 11, 138, 145

Inter-Continental Hotels. 167

Island, The. 61

Jackson, Andrew. 22, *23,* 40, *40,* 81, 88, *88*

Jackson Hall. *43*

Jacobsen, Hugh Newell. 115, *150,* 151, 156

Jefferson, Thomas. 19, 50, 53, 55, 88, 181

Jenkins' Hill. 50, *51*

Jennings, Sibley. 50

John Marshall Park. 26, 42, 141

John Marshall Place. 154

Johnson, Andrew. 31, *31*

Johnson, Hotel. 138, *138*

Johnson, Lady Bird. 13, 42, 117

Johnson, Lyndon B. 11, 120, 126

Johnston, Frances Benjamin. *163,* 167

Jones, William E. 166

Justement, Louis 126

Justice: building, 35, *76;* department, 120, 174, 177

Kan Am Realty, Inc. 153

Kann's department store. 39, 84, 116, *116*

Kaufman's, D.J. 84, 115

Keith's Theater. 86

Kennedy, Jacqueline. 10–11

Kennedy, John F.: Apex Liquors customer, 120; assassination aftermath, 10, 11, 124; and Avenue council, 123; funeral, *92;* on Pericles, 11, 122; reviewing stand, 91; vision for the Avenue, 121–122, *123,* 147

Kennedy, Robert F. 120, 122, 126

Kennedy, Roger. 128

Kennedy Center. 124

Kiley, Dan. 124

King, Coretta Scott. *144*

King, Martin Luther, Jr. 13, 115, *144*

Kiplinger, Austin H. 24, *116,* 117, 121

Kirkwood Hotel. 31

Kronheim, Milton. 160

Krupsaw, David. 118

Ku Klux Klan. 13, *94,* 95

Labor: department, 122; Perkins Building, 44, 127

Lafayette, Marquis de. 160, 181; park and statue, 19, *20*

Lansburgh's department store. 116, 142, 153

Lantz, Michael. 39, *111*

Latrobe, Benjamin. 61

Lausche, Frank J. 128

Law, Thomas. 62

Lee, Harrison. 42, 75

Lee, Richard M. 31, 58, 69, 77

L'Enfant, Pierre-Charles: Avenue vista, 22, 75, 130; career and temperament, 181–182; pantheon,

38, 50, 75; plan, 37, 50–51, 55, 61, 104, 108, 112; sketch, *51;* vision, *53*, 147
L'Enfant Forum. 181
L'Enfant Plaza. 134
Lewis, Delano E. 146, *147*
Lewis Johnson & Company. 77
Liberty Bell replica. 14, 26
Lincoln, Abraham: inaugurals and funeral, 88, 89, 92, 184; IOU, 19; playgoer, 174; portrait, *172;* visits Harvey's, 84
Lincoln Memorial: proposed, 104; reflecting pool, 64
Lind, Jenny. 160, 174
Lindbergh, Charles A. 14, 96
Litwin, Fred, 118–119
Lobbying. 24, 126, 131, 136, 160
Lone Sailor statue. 37

MacArthur, Douglas. 96, 99
McCormack, John & Mrs. 118, *119*
McKim, Charles. 104
McKinley, William. *87,* 104
McLean, Don. 128
McMahon, Robert J. *138*
McMillan, James. 104, 105
McMillan Plan. 104–105, 108, 131. *See also* Senate Park Commission
McPherson, Harry C. 11, 126, 138
Madison, James A. 88
Mall, Washington: Brady depicts, 171; Federal Triangle faces, 112; geometry, 40; L'Enfant's dream, 50; McMillan Plan and, 104; spoiled, 68
Man Controlling Trade statue. 39, *111*
Mankin, Hart T. 126–127
Mansart, Francois, and mansard roofs. 133
Market Space. 39, 77, 116
Market Square: development team, *152;* history, 75, 77; housing, 126, *126*, 151, 153; located, 37; market days at, 76; mixed-use plan, *152*, 153
Market Square North. 153
Marriott, J.W., Hotel. 26, 142, 167
Marsh Market. 75, *111. See also* Center Market
Massachusetts Avenue. 53, 154

May Day, 1968. 119, 121
Meade statue. 42, *136*
Mellon, Andrew W.: board, 108; park, 40; portrait, *109*
Meszoly, Peter T. 135, 136, 137, 151, 166
Metro subway. 37, *72*, 142
Metropolitan Hotel. 39
Metropolitan Square. 22–23
Metzerott Hall. 35, *76*
Mills, Robert. 22, 181
Moore, Charles. 104–107
Moynihan, Daniel P.: and Ad Hoc Committee, 122–123; on architects, 151; on business community, 146; and ICTC, 11; and Kennedy death, 10–11; on the Marriott, 142; on National Square, 128; as Nixon adviser, 127, 133; and Owings, 182, 183–184
Mullett, Alfred B. *78,* 107, 171, *171*
Munsey Building. 26
Murder Bay. 61

Nast, Thomas. *85*
National Archives Building. 37, *37, 75*, 108, *111*, 153
National Avenue. 107
National Bank of Washington. *78*
National Capital Planning Commission. 127, 128
National Endowment for the Arts. 177
National Gallery of Art: East Building, 40, *40*, 42, *154*, 156; gift to nation, 40
National Hotel. 19, 40, *40*
National League of Cities. 140
National Park Service. 131, 141, 142
National Place. 26, 174
National Press Club. *28*, 117, 128, 136
National Square: drawings, 124, *129;* into limbo, 127; model, *125;* Owings on, 182; scorn for, 128, 133; size reduced, 127, 136; unrealized, 128–130
National Theatre: history, 174; located, 26; as magnet, 146; struggling, 117; views, *174*
Navy Memorial: 37, 143, *143, 152*, 153

Nelson, Knute. 107
New Capital Hotel. 43
New Lyceum. 32
New York Avenue. 53
Newspaper Row. 26, *28, 28*
Nixon, Richard M.: Avenue enthusiast, 11, 133; inaugurals, *132*, 184; and National Square, 128; and PADC, *132;* walks the Avenue, 133; Willard headquarters, 165
NS&T Bank. *78*

Occidental Hotel. 24, 84, *96, 178*
Occidental Restaurant. *19,* 24, 123, 128, 178
Oehme, Wolfgang. *See* Oehme, van Sweden
Oehme, van Sweden & Associates, Inc. *141,* 141–142
Office consolidation, federal. 8, 11, 107, 122. *See also* Ad Hoc Committee
Ohio Avenue. 107
Old Ebbitt Grill. *See* Ebbitt House
Old Executive Office Building. 107
Old Post Office Building: demolition plans, 9, 112, *125;* history, 177; located, 31; and PADC, 142; pavilion, 10, *178;* tower, 4, 19, 177; views, *27, 111, 177,* 178
Olmsted, Frederick Law, Jr. 104
One-Two-Three-Four Tavern. 27
Owen, Thomas J. 147, *147*
Owings, Nathaniel: chairs early commissions, 123–124, 126; described, 182; drinking, 182–183; and FBI Building, 127; and housing, 150–151; leaves Washington, 184; and National Square, 128–130; and Old Post Office, 10, 177; and PADC, 134–135; portrait, *125;* and the Willard, 166; zeal for the Avenue, 10, 131, *132*, 142, 181, 182
Oxford Hotel. 24, *24*

Pantheon. *See* L'Enfant
Parades and protests: Armistice night, 96; Bonus March, 96, *99;* circus, *94;* Coxey's Army, 95; Indochina war protest, *120;*

klansmen's, 94, 95 Knights Templar, *161;* Labor Day, *177;* Masons', 55; May Day, 119, 121; paving celebration, *57,* 95; Poor People's March, 13; Poor People's Parade, *114;* Preparedness Day, 96, *96;* Shepherd's, *64;* sleighing carnival, 96; war-related, *88,* 96, *96;* women's suffragists', *83,* 95. *See also* Inaugurals, Funerals
Patent Office, U.S. *53*
Patrick, Mason M. 71
Peace Monument. 44, 44
Peck, Robert. 127, 142, 177
Peets, Elbert. 108, 113, 181, 182
Pei, I.M. 40, *40, 154*
Pennsylvania Avenue: address, 138, 153, 177; animals on, *13,* 14, 19, *24, 43,* 53, 53–55, 69, 75, *75, 94,* 95, 121; architectural laboratory, 14; autos and buses on, *9, 27, 43,* 65, *71, 72,* 91, 112, *119;* bicycles, 95; bird-proofing, 91; ceremonial link, 181; cleaning, *83;* decline, 58, *106,* 114, 115–117, 122–123, 131, 184; description, 13, 55, 81, *106,* 121, 122, *123;* dusty, 55; federal/D.C. boundary, 105; "firsts" on, 77; flooded, 55, 61, 62, *80,* 81; government enclave, 8; as the Grand Avenue, 51; landscaping, *24,* 42, 137, *141,* 141–142, 168; life on, 9, 121, *125,* 126, *136,* 138, 142, *144,* 150, 184; lifts spirits, *144,* 145; lighting, 141; Main Street, 14, 184; mud, 53; name, 53; paving, *40, 57, 57,* 58, 62, 95; pedestrian mall, *54;* promenading on, 81; redevelopment assessed, 8, 184; retail plan, 142–143; seasons, 141; significance, 13, 117, 122–123, 145; sleighing and snow on, *58,* 96, 100; as a swamp, *53,* 107, 126–127; views and vistas, *19, 22, 38,* 40, *40,* 50, *51, 54,* 55, *57,* 61, 75, *105, 119,* 128, 130, *178;* walks along 19–44, 133; wonderfully open, 8. *See also* Ad Hoc Committee, Federal Triangle, Housing, Lobbying, President's Council, Streetcars, Temporary Commission

Pennsylvania Avenue Development Corporation (PADC): "facadism," *32;* and FBI Building, 127, 128; history, *132,* 134–154; plan, 116, 130–131, 134–136, 146; plan map, *147;* and the Willard, 165–166
Pennsylvania Avenue Foundation. 147
Pennsylvania Building. *4,* 116, 138, *138*
Pennsylvania Railroad. *See* Railroads
Pericles. 11, 121, 122
Perpetual Savings Bank. 22, 147, *147*
Pershing, John J. 14, 24, 96, *96*
Pershing Park: *9,* 13, 24, *24,* 130, 131, 137, 141, *141, 168*
Peyton's boardinghouse. 40
Pierce, Franklin. 13, *161*
Pinkerton, Allan. 89
Planning, city. 8, 11
Pocahontas sign. 39, *53*
Poli's Theater. 24, *24, 24,* 113
Polk, James K. 88
Poor People's March on Washington. 13
Poor People's Parade. *114*
Pope, Francis. 61
Pope, John Russell. 108
Post Office Department Building (New Post Office). 27, *111*
Potomac Electric Power Company transformer. 151
Prentiss Properties, Inc. 32
Preparedness Day. 95, *96*
Prescott House Hotel. 26
Presidential Building. 13, 31, 133
President's Council on Pennsylvania Avenue: 81, 105, 112, 123–126, 128, *129,* 134, 135, 183
President's House. 13, 50
Prohibition. 96, *96,* 160
Public Buildings Commission. 107, 113
Public Buildings Service, GSA. 128
Pulaski statue. 26, *27,* 130
Pylons. *See* Western Plaza

Quadrangle Development Corporation. 26
Quesada, Elwood "Pete": 116, 133–135, 137, 146, 154, 166, 184

Railroads: Alexandria & Washington, *66;* on the Avenue, 67; Baltimore & Ohio, 61, *66,* 67–68; operetta, 67; Pennsylvania (and its Baltimore & Potomac subsidiary), 64, 68, *69,* 91, 138; Southern, 205; Tiber route, *60*
Raleigh Hotel. 31, *31, 96, 178*
Reedbirds' Hill. 61
Regan, Thomas J. 131, 137, 141, 143
Rhodes Tavern. 23, *23*
Rich, Frank H. 13, 115, 166
Riggs Bank. 19, *78*
Riggs, George Washington, Jr. 19
Riots, 1968. 84, 115, *116,* 131, 151
Ripley, S. Dillon. 10
Roosevelt, Franklin D.: *92,* 108, *109,* 118, 160; monument, 37
Roosevelt, Theodore: *90,* 91, 104
Roth, T. Christopher. *152,* 153
Rouse Company. 142
Rowe, Libby. 75, 128, 151

S&W Cafeteria. 23
Saint Charles Hotel. 42, *43*
Saint-Gaudens, Augustus. 104
Saint Marc Hotel. 171
Saylor, John. 126–127, 131
Sears House: *65, 78,* 171, *172. See also* Apex Liquors, Brady
Senate Park Commission. 68, 104–105
Serra, Richard. 131
Seventh Street. 115, 142
SHE statue. 44
Shepherd, Alexander R. "Boss". 26, *64, 66*
Shepherd Centennial Building. 31, *31*
Sherman statue. 14, 19
Shipley, Carl. 91, 115
Ship of State float. *90,* 91
Shoomaker's Saloon. *28,* 81
Shouse, Mrs. Jouett. 135
Shops at National Place. 26
Shrago, Jeff K. *147*
Siegal/Zuckerman/Abernathy / Ruben Partnership. 153
Simmons, Franklin. *44*
601 Pennsylvania Avenue. 39
Skidmore, Owings & Merrill, Architects. 10, 123, 124, 127, 182, 184

Slaves and slavery. 42, *43*, 77
Sleep Center, The. 39, 118
Smith, Chloethiel Woodard. 123–124
Smith, Leila. 166
Smith-McMahon Architects, P.C. 14, *138*
Smith, Robert Calhoun. 14, *138*
Smithsonian Institution. 128, 151, 153, 183
Sousa, John Philip. *64*
Southern Railway. *See* Railroads
Southern Railway Building. 26, 86, 113, *178*
Squire Sanders & Dempsey, Attorneys. 147
Stagecoaches. 67
State Department Building, first. 22, *23*
Stephenson, Benjamin F. 39
Steve's Cafe. 120
Strauss Fountain. 112
Streetcars: cable, 69; horse cars, *13*, 69, 77; electric, *13*, 69–71, *71*; snow grounds, 100
Studley, Julien J. 147, *147*
Subway. *See* Metro subway
Sullivan, Louis. 8
Susser, Barney. 118, 119, 120
Sutherland, Asbill & Brennan, Attorneys. *144*, 145
Swampoodle. *60*, 61, 68

Taft, William Howard. 96, 107
Tayloe, Benjamin Ogle. 160
Taylor, Roy A. 136
Taylor, Zachary. *43*, 88
"Tempo" buildings, 10, 11
Temporary Commission on Pennsylvania Avenue: 126–127, 131, 133, 135, 183
1001 Pennsylvania Avenue Building. 32, *32*
Tenth Street. *35*, *80*, *114*
Thirteenth Street. 138, *138*
Thiry, Paul. 50, 123, 124, 126, 182
Thomas, Helen. 13
Tiber Creek and Inlet. 14, 44, *44*, 50, *60*, 61–67, *65*, *80*
Timekeepers, The. 120

Trammell Crow Company. *152*, 153
Treasury: building and terrace, 19, 22, 23, *23*, 128, 130, 181; department, 135, 146
Treasury Square row houses. 24
Truman, Harry S. 121
Turnbull, William. 124
Twain, Mark. 160
1201 Pennsylvania Avenue Building. 27, *30*, 117
Tyler, John. *53*

Uneeda Biscuit sign. 171, *171*
Union Avenue. 107
Union Station. *60*, 61, 68, *120*, 121
United States Hotel. *85*
USO. 14, 40

Van Buren, Martin. 91
van der Rohe, Mies. 8, 182
Van Ness mansion. 61
van Sweden, James A. *See* Oehme, van Sweden
Venturi, Robert. *130*, 130–131, *136*, 142
Virginia Avenue. 53
Virginia Avenue Garden. 141
von Braun, Wernher. 118–119
Von Eckardt, Wolf. 127, 182
Vonhoff, Herman A. 152
von Steuben, Baron. 181

Walker, Ralph. 124
Walton, William. 117, 123, 124, 134, 183
Warwick's Billiards Parlor. 27, *30*, 138, *138*, *178*
Washington & Georgetown Railroad Company, 69. *See also* Streetcars
Washington Building. 23
Washington, George: two hundredth birthday marked, 64; and L'Enfant, 50–53, *51*, 181, 182; Masonic march, 55; sculpture, *44*
Washington, Hotel. *4*, *19*, 22, 24, 118, *119*, 127, 128, 130
Washington Monument. 19, *57*
Washington Post Building. 26, *28*, 81
Washington Project for the Arts. 142
Washington Society of Fine Arts. 142

Washington, Walter. 151
Webster, William. 128
Weiss, Mark. 120, 171
Western Development Corporation. 153
Western Plaza: built, 137; desecrated, 131; festival on, *144*; as Freedom Plaza, 13, *144*; landscaping, 142; PADC and, 130; pylons, models, sculptures on, 26, *130*, 130-131, *136*. *See also* National Square
What is Past statue. 37, *111*
White House: 19, *21*, *21*, *23*, 55, 88, *88*, 146. *See also* President's House, Western Plaza (models)
Whitman, Walt. 44, *44*
Wiebenson, John. 143, *143*
Willard family. 84, 160, *161*
Willard Hotel: congressional fondness for, 166; decline and closing, 115, 165, *167*; dedicated, 142; early history, 160; fire, *162*; lobby and "lobbying," 160, *161*, *163*, *164*; located, 24; and PADC, 142, 166; Palm Court, *163*; Peacock Alley, 160, *163*, 167; razing planned, 127, 128, *129*; Redskins banquet, *164*; saved, 10, 130, 136, 165–166, *167*; suite, *164*; views of and from, *161*, *162*, *167*
Willco Construction Co., Inc. 138, *138*
Wilson, Woodrow. 23, 96, *96*
Wise, Al. 118, *119*
Women's suffragists. *83*, 95
Woodbridge, John. 116, 124, 126, 134–136, 142, 146, 184
Woodrow Wilson Center for Scholars. 151
Woodward & Lothrop department store. 35, 77
World War I. 107
World War II. 120, 121, *164*, *175*
World's Columbian Exposition. 8, 104

Yamasaki, Minoru. 124
Yates, Sidney. 166

Zambo, Lois A. *147*
Zamboni machine. 24
Zouaves, Ellsworth's. *162*

Pennsylvania Avenue:
America's Main Street

Patrons

C&P Telephone, Washington Company
Kiplinger Washington Editors
Oehme, van Sweden & Associates, Inc.
Perpetual Savings Bank
Smith-McMahon Architects, P.C.
Julien J. Studley, Inc.
Sutherland, Asbill & Brennan, Attorneys at Law
Trammell Crow Company
Willco Construction Co., Inc.